The Other Side

Pablo,

I love your desire
for self development.

J. M

The Other Side

Five Rules for Leading
with Influence

JASON A. HUNT

www.i2eyesquared.com

FIRST EDITION: December, 2018

Cover design by Ojedokun Daniel Olusegun.

ISBN: 978-0-578-40736-4

www.i2eyesquared.com

To those who make a positive impact by being on the other side.

Contents

INTRODUCTION

We can all learn to lead.

—Simon Sinek

HIDING FROM EVERYTHING

It was October of 2012, and I found myself hunched over in a dimly-lit portable classroom—you know the kind: a building constructed as a temporary classroom that's separate from but close to the school. This particular portable classroom was not in use, and there I was, hiding, with the lights out and my radio off. Yup, I, the principal of the school, the supposed leader of seven hundred students and a hundred staff members, was hiding like a frightened little child in this portable.

"Hiding from what?" you might ask. Well, everything!

You see, I was appointed principal of this school at quite a young age … thirty-three, to be exact. Sure, when I was initially hired, I knew I could do this job, and honestly, the first year was great. But that changed during year two. Perhaps it was the continual question from parents, friends, and even family: "Aren't you too young to be a principal?" Perhaps it was the series of mistakes that I had unintentionally made in my inexperience. Perhaps it was how I was trying to fill the shoes of the well-loved previous principal who had recently lost his two-year battle

1

with cancer. I don't know. I'm still not completely sure. But one thing was clear: I was scared, and this fear had led me to hiding in a place where I hoped never to be found.

Nothing was going right. I had cut seven teachers to meet district budget expectations. I'd destroyed a long-established schedule based on teaming. I'd required the teachers to work more and prepare less. I'd tried to implement several new initiatives, but with very little success. Our state testing data had plummeted, attendance issues had increased, and the behavior of the students was simply out of control.

When some people experience fear, they run. Others will gear up for the fight. But as for me, I became paralyzed, incapable of taking action . . . similar to a deer standing in the road, frozen, unable to move as the headlights of a car come closer and closer.

In a short time, my fear transformed into anxiety and eventually into depression. I just did not care about anything anymore. I didn't want to get out of bed. My passion for life had disappeared. I wanted to go reclusive and for it all to be over with.

Had I really signed up for this? Is this honestly how my career objective that I had worked so hard and so long for was going to end?

To say I was frustrated would be an understatement. To say that I was disappointed would be stating the obvious. You could definitely say I was stuck, and when you are stuck, you've only got two options: to get up or to get out.

As for me, I seriously wanted to get out. I felt like I could not take on this responsibility anymore. I wanted to leave. However, I have a wife and four kids. We needed an income, and we needed health insurance, so I had to take the other option: I had to get up. I had to figure this leadership thing out, and I had to make it work … not only for me, but also for my family and, as I later realized, for the staff and students of the school.

> *One of the hardest parts of life is deciding to walk away or to try harder.*
> —Anonymous

If you are new to leadership, maybe you've never been in such a situation. Maybe you've never found yourself in a place where all you wanted to do is hide from your responsibilities and where you were stuck, frozen, and unable to move ahead. If you haven't yet, that's great, and I sincerely hope that you never will, which is one of the reasons that I've written this book. However, I've shared this story with hundreds of leaders, and it seems that almost all of them could tell you their own portable-classroom story. It seems that this is just one of the challenges of being on the other side.

THE OTHER SIDE

Imagine a line like that on a soccer field, painted across the grass. On one side of that line are most American workers. These are the technicians, or doers, of our society. You can find them in factories, corporations, the government, non-profits, and almost everywhere that you can find people. Those on this side of the line have important jobs and duties. They work hard, contribute to the greater good, and make sacrifices.

Occasionally, one of these doers has the <u>courage</u> to cross the line. They move from a place of comfort to a place of discomfort, from having rights to taking on more responsibility, from personal results to getting results through the work and efforts of others. We call these people, those one the other side of the line ... LEADERS.

And here is a hard and fast truth about being on the other side of the line: *being a leader is tough*! It's tough because before crossing all your success, all your productivity, all your ability to get the job done was almost entirely based upon your own personal efforts. Once on the other side, your success, your productivity, your ability to get the work done is almost entirely based upon your capacity to work through others and working with humans is a hard thing.

People are unpredictable, emotional, and self-centered. They can bring you the greatest amount of joy one day and leave you saddled with great frustration the next. Often, what works for one person may not work for another. After much effort, you may feel that you've finally won someone over to your side, only to realize that it was all a scheme so that person could get what he or she wanted instead. When you've crossed that line, you've entered a world of challenges.

This was one of the first realizations from my portable classroom experience. Becoming a principal was, for me, the ultimate position on the other side. I had imagined that once I crossed this line, things would be easy. I had observed many on the other side. They made more money, had greater flexibility, and even seemed to not have to work as hard as those they led.

Therefore, when I crossed over the line, I thought I could go at the pace I wanted, that I could do as I pleased. I had imagined that I could tell people what to do, and they would automatically follow. I soon realized that although the other side did come with a nice pay raise, they were not paying me more simply to enjoy the good days. Latin writer Publilious Syrus said, "Anyone can hold the help when the sea is calm." It's when the storm hits that you earn your bigger paycheck, and as most who have been in leadership for any degree of time will say, a storm is always coming.

WHAT THIS BOOK CAN DO FOR YOU

I don't mean to be all "doom and gloom" before you even get into the first chapter. Leadership is actually extremely fulfilling, and I'm not just talking about the money. In fact, I've found that leadership has brought me seven distinct satisfactions in life that could not have come to me in any other way. Here are the seven satisfactions of leading others.

1. Being able to help people grow in an intentional way.
2. Deciding upon an idea with a team and watching it come to fruition.
3. Assisting others to find and use their strengths.

4. Extending my influence to people I've never met.
5. Providing more joy in life for others.
6. Being able to be part of something greater than myself.
7. Knowing that I've made a positive impact in the lives of others.

The purpose of this book is to help you experience these satisfactions as you cross to the other side. If you're like me, you want to start well. You want to look good. You want others—especially those above you—to notice how well you are doing. Plus, deep inside of you is a desire to make a profound impact in the lives of others, and you know you can do this through leadership.

While I cannot guarantee that all of the satisfactions will happen, what I can do is to share some of the most important principles and practices of leadership that I've learned on my journey.

The initial stages of being a leader nearly broke me. My hope, my expectation, my prayer is to provide you some invaluable lessons so that your trip to the other side will be all that you hope it to be.

I am also writing this book because we are in dire need for outstanding leaders. Our world is full of tough challenges, most unlike what anyone has ever seen before. We are closer and more connected than at any other time thanks to social media, yet we are also more divided and unwilling to understand the perspectives of others. Technology has flattened the world, making life easier and the benefits of life more accessible.

However, this has also dramatically shifted the skills, talents, and abilities of what we as individuals and as organizations have to maintain and update in order to stay afloat, not to mention what it takes to stay competitive.

Far too often in today's society, leaders are corrupt, dishonest, and selfish. These types of leaders will not help us solve the challenges of now and the future. The masses are actively seeking leadership from individuals of integrity, those who put people above profits, and those who care to personally and professionally invest in their followers.

Through the Five Rules of Leading with Influence, I hope to motivate and inspire you to become exactly that kind of leader.

Ever since that October day in the classroom, I've dedicated my time, talents, and energy into studying, understanding, and teaching effective leadership. After much research and experience, I have chosen to provide these Five Rules to help you thrive on the other side.

These rules are easy to understand and can be applied by anyone, no matter your current title or position. Each rule is embedded with time-tested principles that are as old as writing itself. Yet you'll find that every rule is just as relevant today as they were five-thousand years ago.

These are the very rules that I applied to my leadership as a principal. It took us two years, but we completely shifted the culture from being extremely toxic, to one of care, support, and growth. When I left the school, to start my own business, the entire staff congratulated me for my leadership in advancing the academic and cultural environment of our school and it was through these very rules that I was able to. The Five Rules have worked for me, and I know that they will work for you.

I encourage you to read each chapter carefully. Take the time to ponder how you can apply these rules to your specific situation. At the end of each chapter, I provide some suggestions to help foster the production of ideas that you can implement.

> *Strength and growth come only through continuous effort and struggle.*
> –Napoleon Hill

Growth is a process, and this book will do you no good unless you develop the process of contemplating each rule, writing down some ideas as to how you could apply the rule in your life, and taking intentional actions in your personal and professional worlds.

It's been said that the greatest gap in our lives is the gap between knowing and doing. While I hope to increase your knowledge and understanding of leadership in this book, my greatest goal is to help you close the gap between what you already know and what you do.

Therefore, when impressions come into your mind, immediately follow them, put them into your calendar, or at the very least, write them in the margins and follow up on them later.

Welcome to the other side. I sincerely hope I can help you in your journey.

WHAT IS LEADERSHIP?

Leadership is the art of getting someone else to do something you want done.

–Dwight D. Eisenhower

L eadership can be quite nebulous. Most will state that leadership is simply getting someone to do something for them, like our thirty-fourth president quoted above. With that in mind, read the following Aesop fable and ask yourself, "In what way is this leadership?"

A Wild Donkey and a Lion entered an alliance so that they might capture the beasts of the forest with greater ease. The Lion agreed to assist the Wild Donkey with his strength, while the Wild Donkey gave the Lion the benefit of his greater speed.

When they had taken as many beasts as their necessities required, the Lion undertook to distribute the prey and for this purpose, divided it into three shares.

"I will take the first share," he said, "because I am King: and the second share, as a partner with you in the chase: and the third share (believe me) will be a source of great evil to you, unless you willingly resign it to me, and set off as fast as you can."

I hope you've answered to yourself, "This is motivation through might and control, and it's not leadership."

So just what is leadership? This is not a new question. In fact, scholars have been asking this question for quite some time.

R.M. Stogdill, who wrote the *Handbook of Leadership*, concluded that "there are almost as many different definitions of leadership as there are persons who have attempted to define the concept," and that was in 1974![1]

Simply do a quick Google search or look for books about leadership on Amazon, and you'll realize that we've added hundreds of new definitions of leadership over the past few decades. Before I provide you with what I have found to be the best and most concise definition of leadership, let me first explain three misconceptions about leadership that many of us learned as kids and need to unlearn as adults.

LEADERSHIP MISCONCEPTIONS

1. Knowledge equals power, and power equals leadership.

I grew up hearing over and over from my school teachers and parents alike the phrase, "knowledge is power." This was one of the main reasons my parents told me I had to go to school. I also knew that leaders have power.

I, therefore, erroneously made the mistake of thinking that if knowledge is power and power is leadership, then knowledge must be leadership.

This error in thinking should have become clear in my college days. There was no doubt that every one of my professors had a great deal of knowledge. Yet, some had the ability to move me, to cause me to think differently, to change me into something better, while others completely bored me. If knowledge really was leadership, then everyone with great depths of knowledge would be a leader.

> I was never the smartest guy in the room.
> –Jack Welch

While it does take knowledge to lead, this does not define leadership.

2. *Only one person can be on the top and being on top makes you the leader.*

I live in Minnesota, land of the frozen 10,000 lakes. During our long winters, it is not uncommon for us to have storms that dump anywhere between twelve and twenty-four inches of snow over the course of a day or two.

Because of this, we Minnesotans have become experts at clearing snow so that we can safely travel to work, school, and the grocery store. The very exciting side effect of this is the creation of large snow hills, which almost magnetically attract kids. What do these kids do once they come to the hill? They race to the top and see how long they can remain alone at the top by pushing all the other kids off the hill (I know, this sounds harsh, but it's quite fun). If successful, they become "King of the Hill."

While this is a fun game, it teaches yet another mistaken understanding of what leadership is. King of the Hill purports that it takes work to get to the top and that it takes work to remain at the top, both true facts. However, King of the Hill mistakenly teaches us that there can only be one at the top, and to keep your position, you must push others down, but not true.

Business expert Tom Peters states, "Leaders don't create more followers; they create more leaders." Those who find it lonely at the top have misunderstood leadership. Instead of pushing people down, leadership is all about pulling people up.

3. Give me a title and do what I say.

Remember playing Follow the Leader and Simon Says? At the core of these games is the fundamental idea that a person has the title "Leader" or "Simon" and that you must follow that person. In the game Simon Says, if you don't do exactly as Simon tells you, you're out. Don't we wish leadership was this simple? "Do as I tell you to do. I am the boss; Whatever I say you have to do; If you don't, you're gone."

This is an error that many people fall into. Leadership simply does not work this way. People with positions and titles are all around us: fathers and mothers, supervisors, managers and bosses, mayors, senators, and presidents. Therefore, it is easy for us to think that as soon as we get a title, we can lead others.

I think that President Eisenhower can help us understand this one better. Remember the quote from the beginning of the chapter? Here it is again, but in its entirety.

> Now I think, speaking roughly, by leadership we mean the art of getting someone else to do something that you want done because he wants to do it, not because of your position of power can compel him to do it, or your position of authority.
>
> A commander of a regiment is not necessarily a leader. He has all the appurtenances of power given by a set of Army regulations by which he can compel unified action. He can say to a body such as this, "Rise," and "Sit down." You do it exactly. But that is not leadership![2]

We've all met "leaders" who push with a title but have no ability to lead. If you've ever had the misfortune to work for such a person, you'll agree that this type of leader only gets three things:

- Minimal effort.
- Momentary change.
- Mediocre results.

If these are the results that you are looking for, then be sure to flaunt that title around everywhere you go. But if you are looking for something more, then you must realize that having a title does not make you a leader.

LEADERSHIP DEFINED SIMPLY

I was on the phone the other day with a potential client. For twenty-five minutes, she described to me her dysfunctional leadership team. After listening politely and trying to get a real understanding of her issue, I responded, "So you've got a problem with trust." There was a pause on the phone, and then she replied, "Huh, yeah, could it be explained that simply?"

After years of being a professional teacher, I've learned the power of keeping things simple. Simplicity brings to us clarity, confidence, commitment, and direction. Sometimes, I think that people take something simple and make it much more complicated than it has to be. If you have ever observed the process of an organization deciding on its mission statement, you know what I mean.

At the end of hours and hours of work, you often have something so long and complex that no one will ever remember it, nor will it inspire them to act. Conversely, think of Nike's "Just do it," the Human Rights Campaign's "Equality for Everyone," or Amazon's "The Earth's Most Customer-Centric Company." These are organizations that understand the power of simplicity.

Although leadership has been defined in a thousand different ways, explaining leadership does not have to be complicated. Defining leadership can be very simple. In fact, it can be defined in one simple word: influence.

I first came upon this word as I was reading the best-selling *21 Irrefutable Laws of Leadership,* by John C. Maxwell. Voted the number-one leadership expert by *Inc., Magazine* and the American

Management Association, John has over four decades of experience working with leaders.

Law Number Two in his book asserts, "Leadership is influence; nothing more, nothing less." Leadership is simply our ability to use our influence to cause people to think or act differently.

Leaders recognize that in order to make change happen, in order to create results, in order to meet their goals, they must develop influence with others. There simply is no other way.

> *The only inheritance that a man will leave that has eternal value is his influence.*
> –Larry Dobbs

Here is a way to think about it: Leadership without influence is like a flashlight without batteries. You've got something to hold (in the case of leadership, a title), but you have no light.

I recall not too many years ago that I was trying to get an entire staff to change a fundamental part of their job. I had developed the ultimate plan, complete with extensive details. I had ensured that the infrastructure of this plan was in place and had shared this plan over and over again with the staff.

After two months of trying without result to get this plan off the ground, I recognized that all I had been doing is holding the title, the flashlight without the batteries. I was using my title to force a change and ignored the rules of influence and therefore was not getting any results. A leadership position without influence is just a wasteful act of holding something that has no power.

As we develop influence with others, we receive batteries for our flashlights and thus can shine a bright light for others to follow.

INFLUENCE: THE WAY TO LEAD

A quick look at almost any dictionary, and you'll find a definition like this:

> Influence (n): the capacity to have an effect on the character, development, or behavior of someone or something.[3]

In other words, influence is our capacity to cause people to think or to act differently. It's our ability to create change in someone, to help a person to think at a higher level, to cause a person to stop doing some things and start doing other things. To do this, to cause change, the best influencers create feelings of uncomfortableness regarding where people are and encourages them to reach new heights.

If there is no need for change, then there is no need for leadership. If we are satisfied with the status quo, if the results we are getting are what we want, then there is no need for leadership, and you can simply ignore the Five Rules of Leading with Influence.

If this sounds like you or your organization, I ask you to consider the following fable, inspired by the work of researcher G. R. Stephenson.[4]

A group of scientists placed five monkeys into a large cage. High up at the top of the cage, well beyond the reach of the monkeys, the scientists hung a bunch of bananas. Underneath the bananas, they placed a ladder.

The monkeys immediately spotted the bananas and one began to climb the ladder. As he did, a scientist would spray him with a stream of cold water. Then, the scientists would proceed to spray each of the other monkeys.

Every time a monkey went up the ladder, the scientists soaked the monkeys with cold water. After a while, when a monkey would start up the ladder, the others would pull it down. Given some time, no monkey would dare start up the ladder, no matter how great the temptation.

The scientists then decided to replace one of the monkeys. The first thing this new monkey did was start to climb the ladder. Immediately, the others pulled him down. After several attempts, the new monkey learned never to go up the ladder, even though there was no evident reason not to.

A second monkey was substituted, and the same thing occurred. The first replacement monkey even participated in pulling it down. A third monkey was changed, and the same was repeated. Again, a fourth and finally a fifth monkey were replaced with the same results.

What was left was a group of five monkeys that—without ever having received a cold shower—continued to pull any monkey down who attempted to climb the ladder.

If we had the ability to ask the five replacement monkeys why they don't go up the ladder to get the bananas, I'm afraid they would answer, "Because that is the way we've always done it." Grace Hopper says, "The most damaging phrase in our language is: 'It's always been done that way.'"

Influencers are agents of change. They are individuals who can help people see things differently. They provide the encouragement and support for them to change, to improve, and to get better. They are people who look up at the bananas and question, "Why?" The pioneer of our contemporary field of leadership development Warren Bennis states, "The basis of leadership is the capacity of the leader to change the mindset, the framework of the other person."

Most in the masses are quite satisfied with how things are. Or, they may be unsatisfied but unwilling to do anything about it. They go about living one day after the next, thinking that their life condition is the way it was supposed to be and that they just need to accept it.

Once we've crossed to the other side, we don't have the luxury of accepting the status quo. We can no longer sit around, complain, and hope that someone will hear us. No, we've now taken on the commitment to not only be dissatisfied with the status quo, but to do something about it.

It's not enough to just idly stand by. You've got to learn what's going on around you. And once you do know what's going on, you are probably going to recognize the need for change. I once saw a bumper sticker that read, "If you're not outraged, you're not informed." Influencers are people on the other side who get informed, become outraged, and use their influence to create change in themselves, the people around them, and the organizations to which they belong.

One of my favorite examples of this comes from a rather short and somewhat reserved woman from Tuskegee, Alabama. Around the turn of the twentieth century, many Southern states had adopted new constitutions that were filled with what became known as Jim Crow laws. These laws imposed segregation in public facilities, in retail stores, and on public transportation. For Rosa Parks, the Jim Crow laws enforced a series of horrific injustices.

Rosa's outrage began when she was a young girl attending elementary school at an underfunded all-black school in Pine Level, Alabama. Rosa recalls watching buses full of white students heading off to their new school, while she and her classmates walked to Pine, as school bus transportation was not available in any form for black children.

> I'd see the bus pass every day ... but to me, that was a way of life; we had no choice but to accept what was the custom. The bus was among the first ways I realized there was a black world and a white world.[5]

For Rosa, this was the moment of learning the status quo, and she saw the need for change. Although she joined the Civil Rights Movement in 1943, it wasn't until 1955 when she was forty-one years old that she decided to take a firm stand. She had seen and experienced too much. For too long, she had stood by as black people in her home state were treated as second-class citizens. Having recently attended the mass for Emmett Till, her resolution to do something was high.

Around 6:00 p.m. on December 1, 1955, she boarded a General Motors bus, driven by the same driver who had once forced her to get off and left her to stand in the rain. Rosa sat just behind the ten reserved seats for white passengers. The bus began to fill up. When the driver noticed that three white passengers were standing, he stopped the bus and approached four African-Americans sitting behind the reserved rows. He then asked the four passengers to get up and move farther back on the bus. Rosa recounted:

> When that white driver stepped back toward us, when he waved his hand and ordered us up and out of our seats, I felt a determination cover my body like a quilt on a winter night.[6]

At that moment, Rosa crossed to the other side. She refused to get up, was arrested, and fueled one of the largest boycotts America has ever seen. Thanks to her courage and her willingness to go against the status quo, our nation changed for the better.

> *In periods where there is no leadership, society stands still.*
> –Harry S. Truman

While our history books are filled with story after story of leaders who gathered their courage and used their influence to make a big difference in our country, you might not see yourself as this type of leader. It might be hard for you at this point to really understand the sort of influence that one person can have on a society, and that is perfectly fine.

In fact, I believe that the greatest examples of leadership through influence are not the ones that school children will study in their history classes. Rather, they are the simple, everyday interactions that we have with others.

Allow me to share a personal example. It was my first year as a graduate student at the University of Minnesota. I was taking a required class called The Principalship. I had been teaching for a few years, had a couple of kids, and had enrolled in a master's program to become a principal. Although I've always been a go-getter type of a person, life had started to wear me down, and I had taken a "just get through it" attitude, especially when it came to my college classes. The professor had noticed this and asked me to stay after class one day. I was curious why, as I was doing okay in the class, had not had any issues, and was flying under the radar just fine . . . or so I thought.

How she influenced me that day transformed my life. It literally put me on a different trajectory, one that would make a major difference in the lives of my family and many others I have talked to.

Interestingly, what she did was not revolutionary. It was mentioned in exactly zero newspapers, and, if asked, she may not even be able to recall the situation. She simply saw a young, aspiring principal who was full of potential but had accepted the status quo. She had the belief that if he really applied himself, he could definitely make a difference. She had become outraged in her own way at the talent that was lying dormant, talent that she knew would continue to go unused without some sort of a trigger, without a catalyst.

On this day, she pulled me aside and said something to the effect of "Jason, I enjoy having you in class. I'm grateful that you've chosen to get your administrative degree. But I'm not that happy. I don't think you're putting in your whole effort, and this makes me upset. I see something in you. I can tell that one day you're going to do great things, but if you merely sit here as a bump on a log, it's not going to happen. Jason, wake up and try to see what you can actually become." And then she walked away.

That day, I became a better aspiring principal. That day, I became a better teacher. That day, I became a better father, a better husband, and a better church member.

Why might she not remember this one conversation when it had such a huge impact on me? Because this was a woman who has lived on the other side of the line for a long time. She has made being uncomfortable with the norm into a habit, one that she acted on each and every day. She truly was an influential leader.

INFLUENCING FOR IMPACT

If you're thinking about this to any depth, you've probably already realized that if leadership is influence, then we are all leaders since we all have. That is to say, we all have influence over people every single day. All our interactions, conversations, and encounters provide us with an opportunity to influence, or lead, others.

Each of these moments of influence has a result, either positive or negative. This result creates an impact on others. **Thus, our influence positively or negatively impacts those that we come in contact with each and every day.**

We can lift another through our words, write a note of encouragement to a loved one, or help someone develop a new skill. In doing so, we are using our influence to create a positive impact on others. Conversely, we can talk about people behind their backs, openly criticize their performance, or simply ignore them as they are speaking, and thereby cause a negative impact through our influence.

In short, at all times, we are influencing or leading people to become a better or a worse version of themselves. Some people find this hard to believe. That is, they don't buy into the fact that they really can have that much impact.

If this is a question in your mind, I ask you to pay careful attention to all of your interactions with other people today. Don't focus on how you are impacting others; rather, pay close attention to how others are impacting you.

- Did their words change your mood, your thought process, your behaviors, or your actions?
- After conversation, were you more motivated or energized to work, or were you drained and depleted?
- Did you have a brighter outlook on life, or was your attitude brought down following the interaction?

If you are honest with yourself, you'll realize that other people have a profound impact on us every single day.

Most of us simply don't pay that close of attention. Most of us live one day at a time, simply going through the motions, repeating the behaviors that we did the day before, and not putting much thought into what our influence is really doing. We then look at our results and conclude that what we are getting out of life is just what we are supposed to get. We think this is what we were destined to have and that "all things happen for a reason." We simply consider our results to be acts of fate.

> *Every moment of life you are changing to a degree the lives of the whole world.*
> –David O. McKay

The Swiss psychiatrist Carl Jung strongly argued against such a line of thought. He asserted that "until you make the unconscious conscious, it will direct your life, and you will call it fate." What I'm suggesting is that we not only bring into an awareness the impacts that we are making on other lives through our influence, but that we also take control of this influence by becoming intentional with it.

If you are in a menial job, a position that is rote or does not require much thinking, you may be able to get by just fine without becoming intentional with your influence.

However, if you aspire for true leadership, if you'd like to make a difference, create meaning in your life, and positively impact the lives of others to the degree that they are thankful for what you have done and how you have done it, then know this: You <u>must</u> become intentional in your influence!

Motivational speaker Simon Sinek says it this way:

> There are many talented executives with the ability to manage operations, but great leadership is not based solely on great operational ability. Leading is not the same thing as being the leader.

Being the leader means you hold the highest rank, either by earning it, having good fortune, or navigating internal politics. Leading, however, means that others willingly follow you—not because they have to, not because they are paid to, but because they want to.[7]

This sort of leadership does not simply happen by accident. To excel on the other side, you must learn how to gain influence and how to use that influence in an intentional way. This book will teach you exactly how to do this.

THE FIVE C'S OF INFLUENCE

Each of the next five chapters is centered on a rule of leadership. I have chosen to call them "rules" because rules are established to help us. They are created to put us onto a pathway of safety and success. Often, a rule starts because someone has done something that resulted in a negative consequence, and a guideline or rule was developed to help others avoid and learn from the action.

Think back to elementary school … most likely, your teacher started the year with some general classroom expectations. As the year progressed, your teacher developed additional rules, like "four on the floor," after a student leaned too far back on his chair and fell over.

As a society, we have a lot of rules like that, most of which we call "laws": buckle your seatbelt, drive the speed limit, use the crosswalk, and wear a helmet.

Why do we have such laws and rules? Because, over time, we have become smarter. We have learned from history, from our mistakes, and from the mistakes of others, and we have realized what is best for our safety and our success. We pass this wisdom on through generations by way of rules and laws that guide them in the right direction.

Another reason I've chosen the word "rule" is that the idea of choice is implicit in the word. That is, we are not forced to follow the rules. It is our choice. If the kid wants to lean back in his chair again, he can. If we want to speed, not buckle up, leave the helmet at home, or cross anywhere we want on the road, we can. It is our choice. However, every time that we violate a rule, we place in jeopardy our safety and success. We can choose to violate the rule, but we must also be ready to accept the potential consequences.

These Five Rules of Leading with Influence have been forged from the wisdom of the ages. They have been proven again and again in the lives of leaders, from the earliest to those currently leading.

The essence of these rules can be found in the teachings of the ancient prophets, the guidance of the great spiritual leaders from the last 2,000 years, and the principles of contemporary leaders. It is our choice to follow them—or to ignore them. If we follow, we will experience great success on the other side. If we ignore, we may still retain our leadership title, but we will find it difficult to influence others to follow us voluntarily.

To help you learn and remember the rules, each rule has a key word that starts with the letter "C" (Character, Confidence, Connection, Collaboration, and Capacity), and each of them includes a principle that can be placed into your mind as a visual (e.g., the Hammer Principle).

Furthermore, the rules are ordered intentionally, based on degree of influence and depth of impact.

In my work with other leaders, I have learned that we all share a common desire: we want to make a positive impact in the lives of others. As expressed above, we make an impact through our influence. Yet, the degree

> *Our degree of influence with someone determines the depth of our impact on their lives.*

of influence that we have with individual people varies; therefore, the depth of impact we can make on the lives of others also varies.

In short, our degree of influence determines our depth of impact.

Let me explain by briefly describing this in connection with each of the Five Rules.

Rule Number One: Character Counts. The primary idea of this rule is that people follow us because of who we are. This rule has the widest degree of influence, as we can impact a lot of people, even those that we don't even know. In 1982, Johnson & Johnson chairman James Burke made a historical decision to recall 31 million bottles of Tylenol after several people died from cyanide-laced capsules.

While this cost the company over 100 million dollars, Burke was praised for doing what was right. His example has inspired many, most of whom he's never met. Our example can provide a model for all those we know and many people we don't know.

This is a very large sphere of influence, yet the actual impact is not that deep.

It's like when we hear an uplifting story or come across a meaningful quote. We like it, and we may remember it, but in terms of impact, it doesn't really change our lives much.

Rule Number Two: Build the Confidence of Others. This rule focuses on our ability to have positive interactions with all those that we encounter, especially those we serve. While you can't give a compliment to a person that you don't know, you can to all those you interact with each day. Additionally, our words—especially as a leader—can have a significant motivational impact in the lives of others.

To say it differently, this sphere of influence is of a smaller degree, but the depth of impact is higher than that of character.

Rule Number Three: Connect Before You Lead. The core of this rule is that to really make an impact in someone's life, you must first connect with that person. You can make an impact on a general level with lots of people through your influence in Rule Number One and Rule Number Two by modeling and motivating them.

However, the next two rules are much more about the individual. The degrees of influence are smaller, but the depth of impact is much larger, and to be granted the permission to go to these inner degrees of influence, you must first connect. Thus, this rule is not necessarily another degree, but rather a link, or a connection, between the first two degrees of influence and the last two degrees of influence.

Rule Number Four: Collaborate to Be Great. Perhaps the primary responsibility of a leader, especially in business, is to get results, and to get results, you need to develop individuals into team players. By using this rule, leaders get to see magic happen when their intentional efforts at developing individuals causes them to live and perform at higher levels.

Obviously, this sort of impact requires a great deal of time. While it is often in a leader's heart to have an impact on all, leaders using this rule focus on groups of two to twelve. This means that the sphere of influence is smaller here, but the degree of impact is much, much deeper.

Rule Number Five: Increase Capacity to Increase Influence. This is the innermost degree of influence; therefore, it has the deepest impact on others. This also means that it is the hardest rule to follow. Leaders at this level purposefully select one or perhaps two individuals to develop into a leader.

Leaders at this level must be humble, willing to sacrifice their own agenda, and be able to come to terms with the fact that those they develop may eventually surpass them in leadership responsibilities. Followers of this rule not only have a deep impact on the persons they are developing, but they are also creating new spheres of influence as the new leaders begin their own journey through the Five Rules.

Below you can find a graphic that puts this all into a visual perspective.

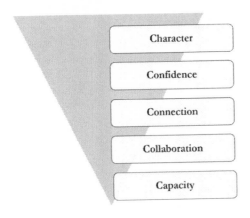

You'll notice that the first rule, Character, is at the top of the triangle. This is where leadership starts. It is also intentionally placed at the widest area of the inverted triangle, meaning that it has the widest degree of influence.

As mentioned, we can influence people we don't even know at this level. Yet, when it comes to a deep change in the lives of others, compared to the other levels, this level has the least amount of impact. Traveling down the triangle, your breadth of influence decreases, but the degree of impact increases. That is, you influence fewer people the further down you go, but your degree of influence is deeper. This means that you can have a more profound impact in their lives.

As I've personally worked through each of these and as I've helped organizations navigate the Five Rules of Leading with Influence, I've come to a powerful conclusion: the further downward you travel, the more time and effort is required. Yet, the further you go, the greater the measure of joy you experience.

What you have heard before is true: the more you put into the lives of others, the more you will get in return. My most satisfactory moments as a leader are not when I've reached a goal; it's not when we've created true change in an organization. Rather, it is when I've helped others develop themselves into leaders and begin to intentionally use their influence to positively impact the lives of others. It's at these moments that all the time, effort, and sacrifice pay off. Certainly, **developing others to become leaders is the holy grail of leadership.**

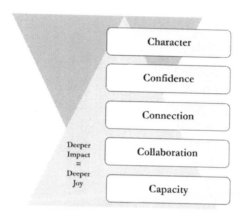

LEARNING TO LEAD

☐ **Determine Your Desire.** Ask yourself, "Why do I want to be a leader?" Take some time to consider this question. Is your desire to be a leader strong enough to do the hard work of leading. If so, read on. If not, stop here and request a short meeting with a few respected leaders in your organization. Ask them why they got into leadership and the rewards they see in leading others.

☐ **What's Not Okay?** Leaders are never comfortable with the status quo. Using the space below, create a list of at least five things that you'd like to change. If you cannot come up with five, stop here and survey those that you serve to see what they think needs to be changed.

_____

_____

_____

_____

_____

☐ **Determine What You're Willing (and Not Willing) to Sacrifice.** If you paid attention to the section on the Five Cs of Leadership, you understand that to have deeper impacts on others, you must be willing to give more up. Make a list below of what you are willing and not willing to sacrifice as you begin your journey on the other side.

Willing to Sacrifice:

_____

_____

_____

Not willing to Sacrifice:

_____

_____

_____

Rule Number One

CHARACTER COUNTS

Nearly all men can stand adversity, but if you want to test a man's character, give him power.

—Abraham Lincoln

Ever since our first family video-game console, we've noticed that our son Eli has a very strong attraction to technology. So, when he got a new Kindle for Christmas at the age of nine, we knew that we needed to take special precautions. Fortunately, the Kindle comes with a password-protected feature for parents, and it can limit the amount of time that a child spends on the device.

Not too long after the Kindle arrived, my wife and I were sitting at a table when Eli came up and slid his Kindle across to us.

We looked up at him with curiosity when he stated, "Dad, you need to change the password on this!"

"Why?" I curiously asked.

He glanced at the floor, shifted his body a few times, and said, "I looked over your shoulder last week and got your password. I've changed my time limits and have been on this way more than you would allow me." Boy, was he right! We changed the password immediately.

A bit later, I got to thinking. Eli didn't show character when he snuck behind our backs, playing longer than allowed on his Kindle. Yet, he demonstrated tremendous character when he admitted to us what he did.

Were we more upset or more impressed? Honestly, we were more impressed by his admission of weakness than anything else. He could have continued to sneak extra time, and he probably would have gotten away with it for some time (admittedly, I'm not the most observant father). But he didn't. He knew that his character was in jeopardy. Even at his young age, he understood the wisdom expressed by writer C.S. Lewis, that character is "doing the right thing, even when no one is watching." He knew that, in the end, character counts!

CHARACTER IS A MAJOR PROBLEM

Although defining character can be challenging, but what isn't challenging is recognizing when its absent. We know it when we see it, and we know it when it's not there. Consider the following examples of missing character from the previous two decades:[1]

- **Ken Lay and Jeffrey Skilling of Enron** — Securities and accounting fraud, conspiracy.
- **Bernie Ebbers of WorldCom** — Accounting fraud, taking personal loans from company.
- **Dean Buntrock of Waste Management** — Fraud, falsifying documents, misrepresenting financial results.
- **Chung Mong Koo of Hyundai Motor** — Fraud, embezzlement, allegedly put money away in a fund to bribe officials.
- **Martha Stewart of Martha Stewart Living Omnimedia and James McDermott of Keefe, Bruyette, & Woods** — Insider trading.
- **Mark Hurd of Hewlett-Packard** — Inaccurate expense reports and alleged inappropriate relationship with a female contractor.
- **John Browne of BP** — Lying under oath.

- **David Edmondson of Radio Shack** — Falsified résumé.
- **Executives at Lehman Brothers** — Subprime mortgage-lending practices.
- **Lance Armstrong and many elite cyclists** — Claimed never to have used performance-enhancing drugs with evidence illustrating the contrary.
- **Jerry Sandusky** — Embroiled in scandal at Pennsylvania State University.

You probably recognize many of these names, and if you don't, you'll at least recognize several of the organizations that they represent.

Unfortunately, weaknesses in character are all around us. The year of 2017 is memorable due to the plethora of sexual misconduct scandals exposed in newspapers, online, and in social media. According to a *New York Times* article, 71 high-profile men have been fired, resigned, or have suffered similar professional fallout due to accusations that are sexual in nature in 2017 alone![2]

This is especially troubling for leaders. According to the research, only 51 percent of employees have trust and confidence in their senior management.[3] Why is that number so low? Again, according to the research, only 36 percent of employees believe that their leaders act with honesty and integrity. And when reporting the last twelve months, 76 percent of employees surveyed have observed illegal or unethical conduct on the job—conduct that, if exposed, would seriously violate public trust.[4]

What this and other studies show is that many employees don't trust leadership. They have heard about and likely have seen examples of leaders who have chosen to do the wrong thing, *even* when people are looking.

While it is easy for me to read through the news and think, "That's not me," upon reflection, I've realized that there have been many times in my past when I was not acting in private as I pretended to in public.

Being a school administrator can be a tough thing. Often, you are trying to make the teachers, the students, and the parents happy all at the same time. At least, this is what I wanted to do, as I believed that if they were happy, then they would like me. As a new leader, I wanted nothing more than people to like me. Unfortunately, this desire caused me to put my character at risk.

For example, I often would get a referral sent to me from a teacher regarding the bad behavior of a student. Sometimes, this referral would be accompanied by the student AND the fuming teacher.

The teacher would detail the infraction with great emotion, and I, wanting the teacher to like me, would respond to her that I would be tough, a strong disciplinarian, and when I'm done with the student, he will be completely different.

Once the teacher left, I dramatically changed my demeanor. It was now the student and me. I would turn to him and attempt to be his buddy. We would talk about the harshness of the teacher, how growing up is tough, and how I should be very hard on him, but since we've had a great discussion, I'm only going to give him a small consequence.

> *The shortest and surest way to live with honor in the world is to be in reality what we would appear to be.*
> —Socrates

He would then leave my office, and I would call the parent. This phone call would include a very brief and often downgraded description of the student's infraction, a quick explanation of the small consequence, and an elaborate discussion on how great their kid is, all in the hope that the parent would like me.

After operating this way a few times and recognizing that it was not good for the teacher, the student, the parent, or me, I changed my ways.

Perhaps you too believe your character is solid. If you'd like to do a self-check, take a moment to rate yourself on the following fifteen-question Character Quiz. You can find an electronic version of this quiz online at www.i2eyesquared.com/resources.

1. Am I firm on my moral decisions, or do I let circumstances change my choices?
2. Do I do what I say I will do?
3. Do I make difficult decisions, even if the decision will adversely affect me?
4. Am I transparent with others?
5. Do I treat people from whom I can gain nothing well?
6. Do I speak negatively about others behind their back?
7. Am I kind and patient with others, even when they are hard to get along with?
8. Do I act differently based upon the person that I am with?
9. Would I act differently if I knew that someone was watching?
10. Do I admit my mistakes and shortcoming without being pressured to do so?
11. Do I try to understand others' feelings and points of view?
12. Am I patient with the faults and weaknesses of others?
13. Do I always put the interests of others ahead of my personal agenda?
14. Do I look for opportunities to serve other people?
15. Do I feel a sincere desire for the welfare and happiness of people?

Taking the time to ponder your own character is a valuable exercise, as a person's character is the first building-block, or cornerstone, to developing a strong foundation of influence.

THE CORNERSTONE PRINCIPLE

You may have walked past an important building and noticed an embedded stone that was different than the rest, usually a little above ground level, near a corner of the building. Often, this stone has a year engraved in it, and if you were present at the completion of the building, you probably experienced a ceremony; where this stone was placed into the wall with a lot of pomp. They call this stone the cornerstone, and these days, it performs no architectural function beyond the ceremony.

Go back a couple hundred years, and there was no more important stone to masonry foundations than this one. Before a building was constructed, a special stone was carefully carved out of rock. It had to be the perfect shape, the perfect size, with perfect edges. This cornerstone was then laid at the future intersection of two walls as the first stone in the entire structure. It became the foundation for the whole building. It had to be set just right; otherwise, you'd end up with crooked walls, a slanted building, or both.

> *Leadership is a potent combination of strategy and character. But if you must be without one, be without strategy.*
> —General Schwarzkopf

Your character is like this cornerstone. It is the foundation for influence. It is the glue of relationships. If you don't have character, no matter how gifted, smart, or charismatic you are, your leadership will not last, and it will come crumbling down.

Thus, the cornerstone principle says this: *your influence starts with a foundation of character.*

One of the greatest examples of this principle comes from a personal hero of mine: Mahatma Gandhi. It's widely accepted that Gandhi was a person of outstanding character, a person who remained firm on his moral convictions, despite very challenging circumstances. Since 1757, India had been ruled by the English, and Gandhi felt strongly that India should be ruled by Indians. He wanted a revolution. Yet, his inner compass said that violence was wrong. Therefore, he faced a mountainous problem—independence without violence. How can you have a revolution without violence? Russia couldn't do it; neither could France, and even the great United States did not gain independence without much bloodshed, so how could Mahatma expect to do it?

Despite the odds, Gandhi led a revolution that gained independence for India in 1947. How? Through nonviolent civil disobedience. He stayed true to the Cornerstone Principle, and people followed him.

OB4S

So, how do you strengthen your cornerstone?

While there are many elements to character, when it comes to leadership, one element trumps the rest. There is one thing that divides the good leaders from the great, one perspective that helps define and direct all the other elements of character. That one thing—the one element that is greater than all the others—is the idea of OB4S, or Others Before Self.

Think of it this way: why do people intentionally violate character? Why do they purposely take a chisel and start chipping away at their cornerstone? Why would people lie, cheat, steal? Why would they hide mistakes, shortcomings, and weaknesses?

At the root of all problems of character is selfishness. People want more money, more power, or more fame. They often want to be seen as givers, but inside, in reality, they are takers. They lack self-control and therefore place themselves above others in every single instance of character violation.

A great example of not placing others before yourself happened in the spring of 2010. British Petroleum (BP) was facing a huge crisis. A leak had sprung on an oil rig in the Gulf of Mexico, eventually dumping 4.9 million gallons of oil into the water. While countless sea animals and birds were dying, families were grieving for lost ones, and residents were trying to figure out how to clean up the mess, BP CEO Tony Hayward was at the center of cleaning up the PR mess. During one interview, he apologized for the tragedy and then stated, "There's no one who wants this thing over more than I do. I'd like my life back."[5] Unfortunately, Tony did not follow the idea of OB4S. This statement displayed a crack in his cornerstone. A few months later, he was replaced.

People that have character are people who tell the truth; they are the same on the inside as on the outside ... people that give instead of take, that admit weaknesses, that don't hide mistakes, and they willingly rely upon others for help. These people have at their very core a belief that others matter.

Rabbi Harold Kushner said, "The purpose of life is not to win. The purpose of life is to grow and share. When you come to look back on all that you have done in life, you will get more satisfaction from the pleasure you brought to other people's lives than you will from the times that you outdid or defeated them."

Consider the example of Tiger Woods. At age twenty, when most people are in their first years of college, Tiger entered the field of professional players. In only one year, he won three PGA tour events, took the 1997 Masters title—with its nice reward of $486K—and became ranked as *the* number-one golf player in the world. For the next thirteen years, Tiger dominated the world of golf. He became a legend, the person to watch and learn from, and his influence touched almost every aspect of the game of golf.

Interestingly, his influence didn't stop at golf. It's a fact that once people become the best in certain areas of life, they not only influence their specialty field, but they can also influence people in areas that have nothing to do with their expertise. Tiger sold cars for General Motors, credit cards for American Express, athletic clothing for Nike, and phone service for AT&T . . . all through his influence.

And then, in a matter of months in 2009, his influence vanished because he violated the cornerstone principle (however, he is making a great comeback – both professionally and influentially).

OB4S really is an attitude adjustment. It's a change in thinking, a mind-shift that takes you from always putting yourself first to always putting other people first.

This can be easy to read, but it is probably one of the hardest concepts of leadership. For most people, the professional working life—up to the point of crossing to the other side—has been full of a "me first" attitude. They've had to look out for number one. They've put their sights on where they want to be, what they want to have, and how they want to accomplish it.

This sort of attitude is not necessarily bad. It is what gives us the motivation to get the education, to apply for the jobs, and to climb the ladder. It is what has caused people to move closer and closer to crossing the line. But once on the other side, the rules change. If your only desire is to move yourself forward, to focus on what you want and where you are, then you are in for a very lonely and heart-breaking journey in leadership.

> *Ability may get you to the top, but it takes character to keep you there.*
> –John Wooden

Helen Keller asserted, "Life is exciting business and most exciting when lived for others." How true this is. And the first step toward an exciting life on the other side is having the self-discipline to change our thinking habits from being centered upon ourselves to focusing on others. You've probably heard the old adage:

> Your thoughts become your words,
> Your words become your actions,
> Your actions become your habits, and
> Your habits become your character.

If we are to change and grow our character, we must first start with our thought habits. British author James Allen said it this way: "A man is literally what he thinks, his character being the complete sum of all his thoughts." OB4S is a change in our thought habits—

from "me" to "you"—and this must happen if you want to lead with influence.

Let me ask you this: how did you pick up your toothbrush this morning? Most likely, this is not something that you thought about. You probably didn't go into the bathroom, look at your toothbrush sitting on the counter and think to yourself, "Hm, I could pick this up with my right hand or my left hand. I think, today, I'll pick it up with my right hand." No, I'm quite sure this was not a conversation that you had with yourself this morning. Why can I say this so confidently? Because picking up your toothbrush has become habit, so it requires almost no thought. For many, selfishness is a habit. It requires no thought.

Tonight, when you prepare for bed, pick up your toothbrush with your non-dominant hand and brush accordingly. It won't take long for you to realize that this is difficult. If brushing your teeth with a different hand is hard, pause for a moment and consider the difficulty of changing a habit of character. What I'm advocating is not an easy thing; however, you cannot lead without it.

THE CASE FOR CHARACTER

Here is how leadership works. First, you get a title. This formal title, while not actually leadership, does give you a temporary degree of authority: people are going to follow you because you are now their leader. Immediately, they start assessing you. They are asking themselves three questions about you. If they say "yes" to all three, they will continue to follow you. If not, your leadership has just ended.

1. Do you like me?
2. Do I like you?
3. Can I trust you?

What does following the Cornerstone Principle do for a leader? It provides a footing for questions one and two and it directly answers question three—and that's a pretty good case for having strong character.

Let's look at the trust question a little deeper. Trust is the lubricant of human relations. It is the bridge that connects people. It is the chain that binds all of us together. With trust, you have a great foundation for successful leadership. Without trust, you may as well turn in your title.

Stephen M.R. Covey, who wrote the book *The Speed of Trust*, said it this way:

> There is one thing that is common to every individual, relationship, team, family, organization, nation, economy, and civilization throughout the world—one thing which, if removed, will destroy the most powerful government, the most successful business, the most thriving economy, the most influential leadership, the greatest friendship, the strongest character, the deepest love.
>
> On the other hand, if developed and leveraged, that one thing has the potential to create unparalleled success and prosperity, in every dimension of life. Yet, it is the least understood, the most neglected, and the most underestimated possibility of our time. That one thing is trust."

Let's go back to the Tiger Woods example. Why would AT&T drop its contract with Tiger immediately following the news of his secret life? Because there are a lot of options out there for phone services, and AT&T has to be seen as a company that people can trust. In fact, one of its core values is that their "daily interactions should start and end with honesty and integrity."[6] Every year, AT&T recognizes that they must influence millions of customers to use and stay with their services. They clearly understand the link between character and trust, and, therefore, dropped Tiger so as not to tarnish the trust they had established with their customer base.

Your success on the other side is entirely dependent upon your ability to create influence with others, and the best way to gain this influence is to establish trust, and the best way to establish trust is to be a person of character.

The Manchester Consulting Firm has found that quickest ways to lose trust are to act inconsistently, to seek personal gain, and to lie or tell half-truths. Yet, if people can count on you to do the right thing, to have the right motives, to make the right decisions, then they will give you their trust, and that means influence.[7]

Character
⇩
Trust
⇩
Influence

FOUR MUST-HAVE CHARACTER QUALITIES

I mentioned before that the single greatest method for building character is placing others before self, or OB4S. In my experience and research, there are four additional character qualities that form the core of character. If you are wondering where to start in leadership, what area to improve in, or what you must be absolutely certain to have, these four character qualities are your answers.

Integrity

Simply defined, integrity is the quality of being honest. It means keeping our promises, telling the truth, and not twisting the facts for personal advantages.

When I think of integrity, I'm reminded of a story about a husband who was very sick.

His wife took him to the hospital, and after many tests, the doctor asked to speak to the wife alone. The doctor then explained to the wife that if she wanted her husband to live, she would have to pamper him, wait on him hand and foot, and not challenge or argue with him. He insisted that her husband needed absolute rest and no stress at all.

On the ride home, the husband turned to his wife and asked, "So, what did the doctor say?"

She responded, "You're going to die!"

I have found that life presents to us many opportunities—often daily—to withhold the whole truth, to tell white lies, and to protect our pride by deceiving others. Avoid these at all costs.

The Center for Creative Research affirms that it is okay to make mistakes in leadership—even big ones—but if you breach integrity, you'll most likely never recover. Do your research, and you'll quickly realize that integrity is a top determiner of success in leadership. A person of integrity sets the moral example for others, and through this moral example, he or she gains influence.

President Eisenhower said this:

> In order to be a leader, a man must have followers. And to have followers, a man must have confidence. Hence, the supreme quality for a leader is unquestionable integrity. Without it, no real success is possible ... If a man's associates find him guilty of phoniness, if they find that he lacks forthright integrity, *he will fail*. His teachings and actions must be square with each other. The first great need, therefore, is integrity.

Here are three actions that will ensure a strong cornerstone in the area of integrity.

1. Tell the Truth.

People of integrity tell the truth. As author Patrick Lencioni states, they avoid "choosing their words and actions based upon how they want others to react," but rather speak the truth.

Early in my leadership, I would sugarcoat the stats. I would only share those pieces that were positive and showed that we were making progress, while hiding the brutal facts. I quickly learned that most everyone already knew the facts, and when I finally humbled myself enough to share the full truth, I quickly gained more respect from my staff. Bo Bennet had it right when he said, "For every good reason there is to lie, there is a better reason to tell the truth."

2. Do What You Say.

People are extremely perceptive and are always on the watch to see if your words match your actions. Management consultant Darcy Hitchock says it this way: "Employees are professional 'boss watchers.' That is, what managers say means nothing, unless their actions model what they say." You've probably heard the phrase, "monkey see, monkey do." It's also true that people do what people see. If you want people to follow you, your words and your actions must be perfectly congruent.

John Maxwell says, "Your talk talks, and your walk talks, but your walk talks louder than your talk talks." When I work with organizations on this principle, I often have leaders take out a piece of paper and create a "Talk / Walk" chart.

On one side of the paper, they list ten things that they have promised to their staff (the Talk). On the other side, they assess how they are doing in fulfilling those promises, using a scale of one to five (the Walk). In areas that are lower than a four, I have them create an action plan that will help them better align their walk to their talk.

Pay very close attention any time that you make a promise, or anything that can be perceived as a promise, and be sure that you deliver. If you can't deliver, don't promise. If you don't deliver, make the effort to explain why. Analyze how well you meet all the expectations that you've set for those you serve. Are you living up to what you expect in others?

3. Speak Positively About Others.

I have some good friends that teach social and emotional learning across the country. At the conclusion of each of their trainings on organizational culture, they have participants take a poll on a few statements, including whether they "honor the absent." This phrase means that when someone is not present, we only speak respectfully about them.

They have done this with over 600,000 people so far, and their research has found that only about 5 percent of the time is this answered in the affirmative. In other words, 95 percent of all the people that they work with openly state that negative talk behind the back of others is a serious problem in their organization.

True, you are a leader, and you'll need to talk about the weaknesses of others, but there is a big difference between "I just can't stand John! The selfish pig always has to have it his way," and "John needs some help with seeing the perspectives of others."

Telling the truth, ensuring that our words and actions match, and speaking positively about others will surely put you on the path of becoming a person of integrity. Once you've done that, you've gained the right to influence others.

<u>Courage</u>

Willard Butch, past chairman of the Chase Manhattan Corporation, gave a speech to a college graduating class and said the following: "You're going to find that 95 percent of all decisions you'll ever make in your business career could be made as well by a reasonably intelligent high-school sophomore." He continued, "But they'll pay you for the other 5 percent." Crossing over to the other side is a public display of the commitment you have to making tough decisions and doing tough things. This takes courage.

Courage means speaking and doing what we honestly feel inside without worrying about what other people think. It's being willing to be vulnerable, to address uncomfortable issues, and to take risks— risks that could even endanger your own career.

> *Courage is the main quality of leadership.*
> –Walt Disney

Church leader Richard J. Maynes relates a personal story about a test for character and courage. His father founded a company that specializes in factory automation. One day, his father invited him on a business trip to Los Angeles to meet with a new potential client. The client was a multi-national company that was upgrading their production lines with the latest in automation technology.

The corporate officer explained that their bid was the lowest bid and, therefore, would be the winning bid. He also explained that not only were they the lowest, but also that there was a significant margin between their bid and the next lowest bid. He further went on to explain that they could re-submit their bid at a much higher price, but still lower than the next lowest. Doing so would dramatically increase their profits while remaining the winner of the bid. All the executive asked in return was a percentage cut of the additional profits.

With this extra money and with the size of the contract, Richard's father could ensure sustainability for his company and all his employees for quite a while. Courageously, however, he turned down the offer and withdrew his bid. On the plane ride back, his father stated to him, "Rick, once you take a bribe or compromise your integrity, it is very difficult to ever get it back. Don't ever do it, not even once."[8]

It takes courage to do the right thing even when no one is looking. It takes courage to make the hard decisions. It takes courage to speak honestly.

Courage is also required to help you become the best. Be honest with yourself—aren't there areas in your leadership and your life where you are weak, areas that do not fall into a strength, or perhaps a skill that you've not yet developed to a satisfactory degree? Certainly, there are, and for you to do your very best, you must have the courage to humble yourself, to admit your weaknesses, and publicly acknowledge your areas of growth. It takes courage as the leader to ask others for help and assistance, but if you can muster up this sort of courage, you'll quickly be on your way to becoming an influential leader.

Empathy

Empathy is the action of understanding. It is being sensitive of and connecting to the feelings, thoughts, and experiences of another. While this sounds pretty soft, and while it contradicts traditional leadership wisdom from a couple of decades ago, empathy has been found to be a key ingredient to succeeding on the other side.

Researchers at the Center for Creative Leadership sampled over 6,731 leaders from thirty-eight countries to understand whether empathy has an influence on a leader's job performance. Their results revealed that "empathy is positively related to job performance." They found that "managers who show more empathy toward direct reports (those who work for them) are viewed as better performers in their jobs."[9]

The chief human resources officer at BetterWorks, who has studied the subject of empathy in leadership, states that "it's one of the most critical capabilities needed to lead and drive employee engagement in a diverse, dispersed, and constantly changing environment."[10]

When people come to feel that we are trying to put ourselves into their situation, to "walk in their moccasins," they recognize that we care for them and that they matter. Treating people with empathy builds relationships, and it helps us establish influence with others.

If you tend to struggle with establishing empathy or if you'd simply like to get better, consider these five keys to using empathy more effectively.

1. *Put aside your viewpoint.*

Try to see things from the other person's point of view. I recall mentoring one aspiring leader who approached me with a professional concern that was also personal in nature. I asked her, "Jane, take your current hat off for a moment and put on the leadership hat. What would you do?"

She instantly responded, "I just can't do that; it's too personal!" She had a lot of work to do in this area.

2. *Listen.*

Listening is such a key element of successful leadership that it will be covered at length in a later chapter. Empathetic leaders are excellent listeners. They restrain judgment, are curious, and ask exploring questions.

3. *Validate the other person's perspective.*

Once you've been able to place yourself into their shoes, to understand why they believe what they believe, acknowledge it. Remember: acknowledging a viewpoint does not equal agreement; it simply is an expression of understanding.

One way that I show acknowledgment when I'm listening to an opposing viewpoint is to use the short phrase, "I hear you." Doing so shows that I care, while not agreeing with the statement.

4. Examine your attitude.

Are you more concerned about <u>your</u> desires, interests, and goals? Are you set on winning, on being right? Are these getting in the way of you taking the time and efforts necessary to truly empathize with others? If so, change your attitude.

5. Ask what the other person would do.

This is a powerful and somewhat subtle way of expressing empathy. By asking other people what they would do if they were in your position, you quickly get an understanding of their viewpoint and the answer that they would most prefer. Knowing this gives you a lot to work with.

American author A. Frederick Collins concisely explained the idea of empathy with this short line: "There are two types of people: those who come into the room and say, 'Well, I'm here,' and those who come in and say, 'Ah, there you are.'"

Responsibility

I grew up in a small town in Utah and found so much value in country living that I've chosen to raise my family in a small town. However, as a thirteen-year-old, I didn't view small towns that favorably. You see, I had a friend who was known for making unwise choices. One day after school, we were walking home and decided to stop by the local gas station. He had just recently taught me what a five-finger discount was—you know, taking something without paying for it—and with his encouragement, I agreed to try it out.

Unfortunately, I was not that good at it, and when we got to the cashier, she asked me to empty out my pockets. I was caught red-handed with a few pieces of bubble gum. She scolded us for a bit and then told us to go home and tell our parents. Do you think I did this? Heavens no, not a chance! I did everything I could do to hide my mistake.

About a week later, my parents approached me and explained how we lived in a small town and how everybody knows everybody—I was caught, and that day, I learned the value of taking responsibility for my actions.

When you step into the role of leadership, you increase your degree of responsibility. You give up a focus on what rights you are entitled to and embrace responsibility for your actions and the actions of others. As we've learned from Spider-Man comics and films, "With great power comes great responsibility."

This can be seen in two different ways. First, you accept that the duty has been placed upon your shoulders to go first, to do what is necessary to move things forward, and to set and achieve goals—to disrupt the status quo. While this can require great motivation, it is the easier of the two things.

The second is more difficult and, therefore, more frequently neglected by leaders, especially those starting out. When you move into leadership, it is imperative to take responsibility for your shortcomings, for your mistakes, and for your failures.

If you are like me, you don't want to make any mistakes. You want others to see you as someone who gets things done, who takes risks that reward, and who has the answers that are needed for present challenges. When this image is threatened through a personal shortcoming, avoid the temptation to hide it or not take responsibility for it. Experienced leaders will tell you that sometimes everything just doesn't get done, that some risks fail, and that, oftentimes, you don't have all the answers. Your job as a leader is to be humble enough to admit this and to be determined enough to resolve it.

> He that is good for making excuses is seldom good for anything else.
> –Benjamin Franklin

One advantage of my portable-classroom episode is that it humbled me. I recognized that whatever I was doing was obviously not working, and if I wanted to be successful, something needed to change. While reflecting, one of my greatest realizations was that I had pretended to be what I was not. I had such a strong desire to be seen as an excellent leader that I often avoided or purposely hid shortcomings. To set things straight, I decided to call a staff meeting. One Tuesday after school, I spent ten minutes with all the staff. I explained to them how I had not been the leader that they needed. I outlined three different areas that I should do better in, based upon their feedback, and promised them that, although I have these shortcomings, I am going to do my best to overcome them. Then I concluded the meeting.

I felt a lot better after the meeting. I felt more authentic, more in tune with who I really was, and I felt a burden lift off my shoulders as I became more honest with the staff. For these benefits alone, the meeting was worth it. But this was just one of the benefits.

Jump forward a few years. It's the second-to-last day of school, and I get stopped in the hallway by our social worker.

"Jason, I'm not sure if I'm going to get a chance to tell you this before school ends, so I'm doing it now."

I was listening.

"Remember that meeting we had where you said you were going to do better?"

Ah … a meeting I was trying to forget. "Yes?" I responded.

"Most likely, you were not aware of this, but that year was the worst year I'd had in my sixteen years at the school. I was honestly ready to turn in my resignation in a few weeks. Your speech, your admission of your failures, and the responsibility you took to correct those gave me hope."

She continued, "I decided to give you and the school one last chance, and I need to tell you that each of the years since then have been wonderful. In fact, this year has been the very best of my entire career!"

That is the power of a leader taking responsibility.

Leaders of responsibility follow the wisdom of coach Bear Bryant. "There are always just three things I say: 'If anything goes bad, I did it. If anything goes semi-good, then we did it. If anything goes real good, they did it.'"[11]

In my experience, I've found the following seven suggestions helpful in developing this leadership quality:

1. Take your current responsibilities as seriously as possible.
2. Do not commit to more than you can handle.
3. Acknowledge your mistakes, and do not make excuses.
4. Never point the finger of blame.
5. Follow through and finish what you start.
6. If you see something that needs to be done, do it yourself.
7. Never be afraid of making mistakes.

After reading these, how are you doing? As a new leader, don't take these four character qualities lightly. Failure to be strong in these areas will lead to certain failure in leadership. Even Richard Nixon, a president who blundered in the area of character, admitted the importance of it while endorsing Barry Goldwater's presidential campaign in 1964. "With all the power that a president has, the most important thing to bear in mind is this: You must not give power to a man unless, above everything else, he has character."

> *Character isn't something you were born with and can't change. It's something you weren't born with and must take responsibility for forming.*
> –Jim Rohn

Recently, I read through a couple of studies that can accurately summarize this chapter. One study examined the effect of an image of a pair of eyes on the contributions to a box used to collect money for drinks in a university coffee room. People paid nearly three times as much when the eyes were displayed compared to a control image that had no eyes.[12]

Another study hung posters of staring human eyes all around the cafeteria at Newcastle University and then studied the "littering behavior" of students for 32 days. These watching eyes cause twice the number of students to clean up after themselves.[13]

Let us not need eyes, real or printed, to cause us to be people of character. Let us make the decision now that we will always do the right thing, even if no one is watching. I think that Thomas Jefferson had it right when he stated, "God grant that men of principle shall be our principal men."

CHARACTER AND DECISION-MAKING

I feel like I cannot conclude this chapter without describing one of the most amazing benefits of having character. In developing your character, you discover values and morals are most important, and you strive to live these daily. This helps you when it's time to make tough decisions, because you've already made the toughest decision: that of living congruent with their values and morals. If you'd like to explore what values you hold the highest, you can find a Personal Values Assessment online at www.i2eyesquared.com/resources.

People without character can be swayed by the opinions of others. They often find themselves deciding one thing today and choosing a different thing tomorrow. They have no solid ground to stand on, so they go wherever the shifting sands lead them. They are easily influenced, change their minds often, and have little conviction.

People of character use their predetermined morals and values to make decisions. It's like when you were in high school and they taught you to "Just Say No." What were they doing? They were teaching you to make a moral decision even before that decision was before you. Doing so makes it so much easier to "Say No" when the time of temptation does come.

People of character don't worry about what others will think, because they have the satisfaction of knowing that their decisions align with their morals and values. They also are not easily swayed from their decision because of their character. The great leader Napoleon Hill expounded upon this idea when he said, "Men who succeed reach decisions promptly and change them, if at all, very slowly. Men who fail will reach decisions, if at all, very slowly and change them frequently and quickly." Men and women who do this can because they've developed and strengthened their cornerstone.

Steve Jobs added to this in a very realistic way. He said, "Remembering that I'll be dead soon is the most important tool I've ever encountered to help me make the big choices in life. Because almost everything—all external expectations, all pride, all fear of embarrassment or failure—these things just fall away in the face of death, leaving only what is truly important," and what is truly important is character. Decide to be a person of character and become firm in your decision-making.

STRENGTHENING THE CORNERSTONE

☐ **Take the Character Quiz.** Assess your character by using the Character Quiz. Identify two areas of strength and two areas for growth. List these below and make a plan to improve in each. Get a more comprehensive understanding of your character by having a few people you trust take the quiz about you.

Areas of Strength:

1. _____

2. _____

Areas of Growth:

1. _____

2. _____

☐ **Give Up to Go Up.** Determine now to be a leader who puts OB4S. Find a cheap journal and write in it at the conclusion of each day. Specifically, reflect on what you have given up during your day to help someone go up.

☐ **Rate the Fake.** If you'd like to strengthen your ability to be authentic, try to Rate the Fake. After each conversation you have with an individual, rate on a sheet of paper how "fake" you were in your conversation. A 1 would be completely fake, while a 10 would mean that you were absolutely transparent with the other person. Do this for each conversation you have over the next two weeks.

☐ **Do a Daily Darn-Hard Deed (The Triple D).** It's been said that leaders get comfortable being uncomfortable. Having a strong cornerstone means having the courage to take bold actions and to stand up to the pressure of outside forces. To develop this courage, find one thing <u>each day</u> that stretches you outside of your comfort zone. It could be providing critical feedback to someone, taking a stand on an issue, presenting an idea to a higher up, or seeking feedback on your own performance. Follow this and you'll see your courage increase.

Rule Number Two

BUILD THE CONFIDENCE OF OTHERS

Leadership includes both what you do and what you leave . . . and the most important thing you can leave are people who have increased in capacity and confidence.

—David A. Bednar

Not long ago, I traveled to Rochester, Minnesota, to enjoy a TEDx event. Each of the speeches was mesmerizing, but the one that really caught my attention was given by a what seemed like a very confident and successful man in his late twenties. His introduction was captivating and he was doing a great job when suddenly, mid-message, he shifted gears and began to express his true feelings: how he didn't feel like he deserved to be on that stage; that there are many others who are more capable, more able, and more deserving of a spot at this prestigious event; and how he felt like an imposter. This caught me off guard, as he didn't seem like an imposter at all to me.

The reason that this, out of all the other talks, caught my attention is that I too have felt this way before. In fact, I feel this way all the time. When I was a principal, the thought that repeated in my mind was, "What gives you the right to lead here? There are many others that are better, many that exceed your ability and years of experience in education, so why you?"

This line of thinking made sense when things were not going well, but surprisingly, this thought continued to pop into my mind even when I knew that my leadership was doing amazing things. The same sort of thought has hit me as I serve in leadership positions at church and even now while I travel around as a speaker and trainer. No matter my life circumstances, the exclamation "You're not good enough for this!" continues to enter my mind.

EVERYONE STRUGGLES

This got me thinking. If this TEDx speaker struggles with these feelings and so do I, then who else struggles? Well, it turns out that almost everyone does. According to Dr. Joe Rubino, who wrote *The Self-Esteem Book*, 85 percent of the world's population struggles with thoughts of self-doubt, even "many very successful businesspeople."[1]

Interestingly, this is true even at the highest levels. Believe it or not, both our sixteenth president Abraham Lincoln and our twenty-sixth President Teddy Roosevelt suffered from a lack of confidence.

Teddy was born a sickly child who battled asthma. While he was a kid, he was nervous and timid and had to go through many years of a strenuous physical exercise program to gain confidence. It's also a well-documented fact that, in 1836, Abraham Lincoln had an emotional breakdown and was bedridden for six months due to a lack of self-confidence following several political failures.

Modern-day heroes also struggle. Consider two stars who exhibit great amounts of confidence on screen and in interviews, but who have publicly expressed their struggles. Will Smith admits, "I still doubt myself every single day. What people believe is my self-confidence is actually my reaction to fear."

Famous *Tomb Raider* actress Angelina Jolie has revealed that she spent years in her childhood struggling with an eating disorder, taking every drug you can think of, engaging in self-harming practices, and she even tried to commit suicide on more than one occasion. You can be sure that a low degree of self-confidence was a huge part of those problems.

Even world-renowned author and civil rights activist Maya Angelou expressed, "I have written 11 books, but each time I think, 'Uh oh, they're going to find out now. I've run a game on everybody, and they're going to find me out.'"

If these highly successful people have struggled with self-confidence, imagine how hard it may be for those that you work with each and every day!

IT'S NO WONDER

We live in a negative society.

Simply turn on the news and count the number of positive stories as compared to the number of negative ones. Pay attention to any parent, and you'll hear the word "no" much more frequently than "yes." Play an hour of pop music and count how many lyrics promote self-confidence, compared to tunes that degrade, damage, or outright destroy self-image.

It's intriguing to note that even when we are among friends having a good time, our most frequent expressions to each other are sarcastic put-downs. Take, for example, a group of teenage boys waiting after school for their sports bus.

"Is that your real face, or are you still celebrating Halloween?"

"Why don't you go into that corner and finish evolving?"

"Look, it's great to donate your brain to science, but shouldn't you have waited 'til you're dead?"

These are real lines that I've heard from boys that are the best of friends and that care deeply for each other. It's no wonder that the number of cases of diagnosed depression are up, that suicides are climbing each year, and that almost everyone struggles with self-confidence![2]

THE HAMMER PRINCIPLE

For a person who has recently crossed to the other side, understanding what has been written in this chapter thus far is not only extremely essential, it's also the key to leading other people.

Once you've received a title, you are given a place of critical importance regarding one's confidence. What you say and how you say it can lift people up, can heal people, and can provide the building blocks for helping people to perform their very best. Yet, you also have the ability to tear people down, to cause deep harm, and to destroy the very foundations of their confidence. As a leader, people look up to you and put more value on what you say than what their peers or sometimes even what their families say.

Let me relate your influence on others to a hammer. Early in my youth, I learned the craft of being a handyman from my father. Probably THE most important tool for any handyman is the hammer. Not long ago, I built a Hilton-style chicken coop (at least that's what my father-in-law calls it). I could not have provided these living quarters for our backyard chickens without a hammer; it was fundamental to the proper construction of the coop. With the hammer, I built something beautiful, something that others could enjoy.

Compare this to the other day when I was preparing the floor of a kitchen for tiling. It was a hammer that I used to tear off all the molding. It was a hammer that I used to rip out the transitions from the linoleum to the carpet. It was a hammer that I used to dig into the linoleum to remove it. In this instance, a hammer was used to destroy.

The hammer principle says this: *Your influence will build people up or tear people down.* Every interaction, every conversation, every decision is one that can be used to create, uplift, and motivate those you lead, or to destroy, lower, and de-motivate those very same people—and if you're paying attention, you'll quickly realize that there needs to be much more building and much less tearing down.

> *Leaders relentlessly upgrade their team, using every encounter as an opportunity to evaluate, coach, and build self-confidence.*
> —Jack Welch

This principle may contrast with what you believe a leader is supposed to say and do. Perhaps, when you think of leadership you imagine a person of power who is not afraid to crack the whip. A person who tells things like they are, who doesn't hide the brutal facts, who belittles and beheads until what they want is achieved. While there certainly is a place and a time to be stern, and often exposing the brutal facts is beneficial, how we do this can make the difference between people seeing us as brutal dictators or influential leaders.

As I mentioned in an earlier chapter, you can choose to dictate through your title, but you'll only get three things: 1) minimal effort 2) momentary change, and 3) mediocre results.

In addition to this, people won't like you, they will talk about you behind your back, and you'll end up spending all your time trying to fill positions rather than moving your organization forward.

Conversely, if you focus first on the person and then on the issue, if you keep in mind that everyone struggles and what you say can help a person through his or her struggle, and if you intentionally take the time to praise, reward, encourage, and provide hope, you'll get followers that will go to their death for you. Truly, the world is looking for hammers that build, not destroy!

CAN YOU SEE?

If you'd like to be a hammer that builds, here is a very important concept to understand: you cannot add value to people if you don't see value in people. Let me state that again: **you cannot add value to people unless you see value in people.** Let's take a simple test to help us learn this concept. Read the following sentence:

FINISHED FILES ARE THE RESULT OF YEARS OF SCIENTIFIC STUDY, COMBINED WITH THE EXPERIENCE OF YEARS.

Now look at the sentence again and count the Fs in the sentence. Count them ONLY ONCE. Don't go back and count them again. Keep this number in mind as you read on.

Imagine this sentence to be the people that you are leading and you are trying to determine who they are—that is, their strengths, their current capacity, and what value they can add to the organization. Upon first look, we often make judgments, we assess people (usually in only a matter of minutes), and these assessments become cemented into our mind.

In other words, our judgments become the basis of our belief in people, and in most cases, when we've established a belief about a person, we rarely change it.

This is especially valuable to understand when considering our interactions with others. Why? Because our beliefs drive our behavior. That is, what we believe about a person, consciously or subconsciously, drives our behavior with that person. If we see the person as a lazy, self-centered individual, we will treat that person in accordance with this view. If we see someone as a driven, self-disciplined individual, we will also treat that person according to our perception.

But what if we are not seeing correctly?

Think of the number of Fs that you counted earlier. I've done this exercise with hundreds of people. When I ask them how many Fs they saw in the sentence, most (65 percent or so) will respond that they saw three and only three Fs. Is that you? If so, let's consider you as average in your ability to assess the number of Fs.

The slightly-better-than-average will see four or five Fs. The genius will spot that there are actually six Fs in the sentence. If by chance you didn't see all six, don't beat yourself up. Naturally, we skip articles or small prepositions (such as "of"), and the word "of" has a "V" sound instead of an "F" sound. Furthermore, you were not wrong—there were three Fs; you just didn't see the other three Fs.

For us to be a hammer, we need to constantly be looking for more Fs. We need to frequently question ourselves and ask, "Am I seeing all that there is to see with this person?" As you do this, you'll start to see more. You'll recognize that all people have gifts, all people have strengths, and all people can grow. When you see this, you can start to add value because you see value; you can become a hammer that builds.

> *Great leaders inspire people to have confidence in themselves.*
> –Eleanor Roosevelt

Consider the following story written by an unknown author of a teacher that used her hammer to build and the effects it had on a young boy named Teddy:

On the first day of school, Mrs. Thompson stood in front of her fifth-grade class and told the children a lie. Like most teachers, she looked at her students and said that she loved them all the same.

That was impossible though, because in the first row, slumped in his seat, was a little boy named Teddy Stoddard.

Mrs. Thompson had watched the year before and noticed that he didn't play well with others, that his clothes were messy, and that he constantly needed a bath. Oh, and he could be quite unpleasant!

In preparing for the year, Mrs. Thompson could imagine the struggles. She knew that she had to come out on top, and so she started preparing for the battle (she was seeing the three Fs and didn't like what she saw).

At the school where she taught, it was required to review each child's past records, and she put Teddy's off until last.

However, when she did review the file, she was greatly surprised. Teddy's first-grade teacher wrote, "Teddy is a bright child with a contagious laugh. He does his work neatly and has good manners ... he is a joy to have in class." Yet, during second grade, his mother became terminally ill. During third grade, he started to struggle due to his mother's death and lack of support from his father. During fourth grade, he struggled, had few friends, and slept often in class.

By now, Mrs. Thompson realized the problem (she found more Fs), and she was ashamed of herself. She felt even worse when her students brought her Christmas presents, wrapped in beautiful paper and tied with pretty ribbons, except for Teddy's. His present was clumsily wrapped in a heavy, brown paper bag that he got from the grocery store.

Deep inside, Mrs. Thompson could see value in Teddy, so she took the pains to open the present in the middle of the other presents. Some kids laughed when she found a rhinestone bracelet with missing stones and a perfume bottle that was only quarter full. She ignored the laughs, put on the bracelet, and dabbed some of the perfume on her wrist. Teddy stayed after school to tell her, "Mrs. Thompson, today, you smelled just like my mom used to." She cried for an hour after he left.

Mrs. Thompson continued to pay attention to Teddy. As she worked with him, his mind seemed to come alive. The more she encouraged him, the faster he responded. By the end of the year, Teddy had become one of the smartest children in the class.

A year later, she found a note from Teddy under her door. "You're the best teacher I've had in my whole life." Six years went by before she got another note from Teddy. He wrote that he had finished high school, third in his class, and she was still the best teacher he'd ever had.

Four years after that, she got another letter, saying that while things have been tough at times, he stuck it out and would soon be graduating college with high honors. Four years after that, she got another letter stating that she was still his favorite teacher, signing his name, Theodore F. Stoddard, MD.

The story doesn't end yet. Later that spring, there was yet another letter, one that stated that his dad had passed away, that he was to be married, and that if she would, he'd like her to stand in for his mom at his wedding. Of course, Mrs. Thompson did.

And guess what? She wore that bracelet, the one with the missing stones. And she made sure to wear the perfume. They hugged each other, and Dr. Stoddard whispered in Mrs. Thompson's ear, "Thank you, Mrs. Thompson, for believing in me. Thank you so much for making me feel important and showing me that I could make a difference."

Mrs. Thompson didn't see all the Fs in the beginning. Yet, she took the time to learn and understand, and because she learned to see the value in Teddy, she could also add value to him.

REFRAME YOUR MIND

The act of seeing things differently than we currently do is called cognitive reframing by psychologists. For many, cognitive reframing is when individuals view serious life experiences in a new way. This can be used to help someone cope with a loss by seeing the positives that come from the loss, such as the reunification of family members that you've not seen for years.

> *When you change the way you look at things, the things you look at change.*
> –Wayne Dyer

Cognitive reframing can also help us change how we see people. If we've made negative judgments about persons, we can use this strategy to improve how we see them.

Let's go back to Mrs. Thompson and say that she didn't take the time to read through Teddy's files. Her view of Teddy would be fairly negative. Her thoughts about Teddy would lead to certain beliefs about him and his ability to perform. This negative feeling would create action (perhaps using quick, sarcastic remarks toward him or laying down the rules like a dictator), and her actions would get results (a rebellious kid whom she sends to the principal). The results would then confirm her first thoughts, and the cycle would begin again.

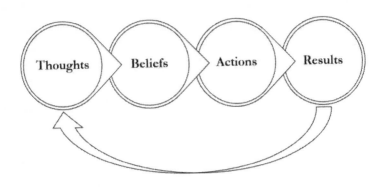

Perhaps Mrs. Thompson becomes unsatisfied with the result (or her principal tells her that he's tired of seeing Teddy). She could change her actions: she could pretend to be nice; she could give him a reward or two; or she could ask him some questions about himself. This would result in a little positive change, which is typical when all we do is change our action. Why? Because Teddy's smart and would easily be able to see through the actions and recognize that, internally, she doesn't care, that she still thinks of him as a worthless, good-for-nothing troublemaker.

The focus in cognitive reframing is on changing how we think about things: that is, how we see or view something, not what we do. Steven Covey says, "I have found that if you want to make slow, incremental improvement, change your attitude or behavior," or in reference to the model above—change your beliefs or actions. He goes on to say, "But if you want to improve in major ways—I mean in dramatic,

> *You can't make the other fellow feel important in your presence if you secretly feel that he is a nobody.*
> –Les Giblin

revolutionary, transforming ways—if you want to make quantum improvements, either as an individual or as an organization, change your frame of reference"[3] (in other words, change the way you think about things). Our actions are simply byproducts of our belief systems that are created through how we think about things.

Leaders who build recognize that the first step in changing someone is changing what they think about that person. Only then will they be authentic in their actions toward changing someone. We must reframe our minds.

EIGHT METHODS FOR BUILDING CONFIDENCE

Reframing our minds is not an easy thing to do. Again, we are creatures of habit, and we probably have belief systems that are potential obstructions to our ability of being a builder of confidence in others. Yet leaders don't allow their belief systems to inhibit their ability to make a positive impact through their influence for long. These kinds of leaders—these builders—consistently carry out the following eight actions.

1. Builders Become Close to Those They Serve

When I started out in leadership, I was often warned by those more experienced than I that I should never get too close to "the followers." Besides, if I do, it might make firing the person that much harder.

I'd argue that 1) firing is always hard, and if you find it easy, then you need to go back and read the character chapter; and 2) it is much easier to do everything, including letting someone go, when you've established a close relationship.

Now, I don't advocate going out to drinking parties with those you lead, but I do know that you can't develop a relationship of influence unless you break down the barriers and allow yourself to get close to those you serve. Give them your time, walk among them with no agenda, get to know details of their personal lives, and let them get to know you. I once gave a person the pink slip a week before his wedding. I had no choice on timing due to district guidelines, but it wasn't as hard as it sounds, due to our close relationship.

2. Builders Ask for Opinions

This is such an easy method that is often underutilized. What hurt can it do to go and ask the opinion of two or three of those you serve about a decision you are considering? Even if you don't go along with their suggestions, you've lifted them higher by giving them a chance to have input. You've expressed your value of them by taking the time to value their opinion. I keep in mind the short phrase "ask two before I do," meaning that I ask two people their opinions before I make decision.

3. Builders Make Themselves Accessible

Most likely, you are a little further down the road than those that you lead. Do you remember what it was like when you first started? Can you recall your struggles, your questions, your desire to have a go-to person? Let people know that you are there to help them. Provide to them office hours when you are open to talk to anyone or let them know the process by which they can get your time. Although you may be higher than them on the organizational charts, they want to know that you are not unreachable and that they can come to you for guidance.

4. Builders Believe Before They Succeed

When it comes to those you lead, don't be a fair-weather fan. Don't be the person that only believes in others when they are doing well and who talks poorly about them when things are not going well.

Give them your honest belief that they can grow, improve, and become great. Clinton Duffy, an American prison warden in the '40s and '50s who led the prison-rehabilitation effort, was often attacked by critics. One such critic said, "You should know that leopards don't change their spots!"

To which he replied, "You should know that I don't work with leopards. I work with men, and men change every day." A building leader believes that people can change.

5. Builders Bestow Opportunities

Like asking for their advice, providing people an assignment or opportunity shows your confidence in them, which helps boost their confidence in themselves. Find jobs and tasks that are not menial but important and schedule a meeting with a person you serve. Help them see how important the job is by showing them how it fits in the big picture and then assign it to them. You'll find that people will respond positively to this type of request. More on this in the capacity chapter.

6. Builders Help Others Succeed

There is nothing that can build one's confidence as well as success. Competence and confidence go hand in hand. Provide the support necessary to help them be successful, even if it is something small. Share with them your experiences, educate them, send them to conferences, give them books to read, and help them work on their personal development.

7. Builders Bring Learning to Failure

For the most part, I think that our society misunderstands the word "failure." Many that I know strive to avoid failure at all costs. Yet, this is not what life teaches us.

Think about it: when have you grown the very most in your life? Has it been the good times or the times that hurt the most? Although my portable classroom experience was terrifying, it also provided to me one of the greatest learning experiences of my life. Yoda has it correct when he says, "The greatest teacher, failure is."

Simply contemplate for a moment how you got to where you are now. How many times did you have to fall before you learned to walk? How many times did you use bad past tense ("waked up," "goed") before learning to speak correctly? How often did you mess up relationships before you finally figured it out and found "the one"? Some of us are still working on those last two.

I once heard that the people most successful at bouncing back view failure not like a cancer, but instead more like puberty: awkward and uncomfortable, but a transformative experience that precedes maturity.

> Only those who dare to fail greatly can ever achieve greatly.
> –Robert F. Kennedy

Success is not achieved by avoiding failure, but rather the pathway to success is paved with the stones of failure. Leaders who help others find the learning in each failure are leaders who build. Help those you serve to realize that all who have achieved great success have only done so by embracing and learning from failure.

Here is a short list of my favorite failures of highly successful people:

- **Soichiro Honda** was turned down by Toyota during a job interview for an engineering position (Yes, THAT Honda).
- **Stephen King's** first book, *Carrie*, was rejected 30 times before he threw it in the trash. His wife saved it and urged him to follow through.
- **Oprah Winfrey** was fired from her television reporter job because she was "unfit for TV."
- **Charles Shultz**, creator of the *Peanuts* comic, was turned down by his high-school yearbook.
- **Dr. Seuss** was rejected by 23 publishers. The 24th attempt sold 6 million copies.
- **Walt Disney** was told, "It's easy to see from these sketches that you have no talent."
- **John Grisham** took three years to write *A Time to Kill,* and it was rejected 28 times. He has now sold over 250 million copies of this book.
- **Harland David (Colonel) Sanders'** fried chicken recipe was rejected 1,009 times before his KFC dream became reality.

Simply by studying the lives of successful people, we can acknowledge that rather than running from failure, we should consider ourselves lucky and celebrate failure—we are now in the company of the very best.

As you read this, your attention may be focused on you and your failures. Let's shift that thought for a moment and think about the failures of those you lead.

Knowing that "success consists of going from failure to failure without the loss of enthusiasm,"[4] how have you responded to their failure? Have you belittled them? Have you made them feel even worse than they already felt? Have you increased the hurt, causing them to say to themselves, "Gosh, I'll never try something new again!"? Or have you celebrated the failure? Have you sat with them and said, "Bummer, that didn't go as planned. What do you think you can learn from this? What will it take to move forward?"

Celebrating failure shows others that you care more about the person than the task. Celebrating failure allows people to feel secure to leave their comfort zones. Celebrating failure encourages people to take risks and to grow.

8. Builders Give Hope

In short, each of these methods are doing one thing: they are showing to the other individual that you have hope in them, that you believe in their abilities. Napoleon Bonaparte, one of the world's greatest leaders, shared, "A leader is a dealer in hope." You should strive to be a hope dealer. With hope, people grow. Without hope, people stagnate.

There's a story of a New York City businessman who was late for the subway. He ran down the stairs to catch his train and noticed a homeless man sitting against the wall. Being the charitable person he was, he stopped for a brief moment, quickly opened his wallet, and threw a couple of dollars into the beggar's hat, then hopped onto the subway just in time.

As the doors were closing, a thought struck him, and he threw out his hand between the closing doors. He got off the subway, went back over to the beggar and said, "I'm sorry. I noticed you are a businessman. You're selling pencils at a very reasonable price, and I have not treated you as I should have. May I have the pencils that I've purchased?" Somewhat shocked, the beggar then handed him a couple of pencils, and the businessman caught the next subway train.

Four months later, the same businessman was attending a networking event, when an older gentleman in a nice suit approached him. He stretched out his weathered hand, and as they shook, he stated, "You probably don't remember me, but I will never forget you. I was that beggar in the subway station selling pencils. That day, you gave me back my dignity. You reminded me of who I really am and what I can be. I have a good, steady job now and am restoring the confidence I once had. Thank you!"

> *A person who, no matter how desperate the situation, gives others hope, is a leader.*
> —Diasaku Ikeda

Let's decide right now to be a leader who uses our influence to build others up, to create, to support. Let's be a builder of confidence.

TEAR DOWN TO BUILD UP

While I've spent the entirety of this chapter advocating for you to be a leader who builds, there are a few occasions when you must tear down. In the work of leadership, sometimes you must tear down to build up. This is especially true when it comes to giving feedback to those you serve.

Giving positive feedback is easy and fun, and it should be done frequently. Much of what I have written in this chapter urges you to do so. I find myself doing this all the time: complimenting an individual for work well done, sending off a written card with a word of encouragement, crafting an email describing how one has had a positive impact on me, or purchasing a small gift to show someone my love. I get great satisfaction from doing so.

It's the opposite of positive feedback that is difficult, and it's difficult, because it means you have to tear down. Call it what you will—constructive criticism, judgment, evaluation, feedback, etc.—telling people that they can improve is never easy.

In all my work with leaders, this seems to be the most difficult task of leadership. Many leaders tend to ignore, avoid, and delay feedback. Some run from it like it's the plague. Most will do it, but only when required to do so or when the actions of another have become so damaging that they must address the issue in order to prevent more problems.

Unfortunately, if you fall into the trap of only providing feedback when required, not only are you violating the cornerstone principle by not demonstrating courage, but you are also stunting the growth of those you serve.

How can people grow if they don't know how they are doing? How can they develop, when they can't see their blind spots? How can they improve if they've not been shown how? Providing feedback gives you the opportunity to help someone rise to a higher level, to help that person perform better than he or she thought was possible.

Not too many years ago, I joined a gym. The primary reason for doing so was to have a place to run that was not twenty below. One day, after suffering through the boredom of running several miles on a treadmill, I decided to lift some weights.

Please understand, I'm a tall, skinny dude and have been my whole life. Because of this, I've often had "tank envy," meaning I'm envious of guys that look like a tank. Yet, I've never really attempted to bulk up. After a few short reps on the bench, I decided that I wanted to give my best effort to building muscle.

Over the next year-and-a-half, I gained twenty-five pounds of muscle. To do so, I not only spent a lot of time in the gym, but I also spent a lot of time learning about how to build muscle. The first thing that I learned about muscle-building is that to build, you must first tear down. At first, that did not make a lot of sense to me. Then, after following a specific program for a few weeks, I started to see growth. I'd go to the gym and rip apart my muscles by pushing as much weight as I could for a short number of reps.

When finished, I would pack my body full of nutrition—high-protein foods, shakes, milk, fruits, vegetables, and carbohydrates. Each evening, I'd lie down to sleep, and while I was sleeping, my body used the nutrition to build back and strengthen the torn muscles, giving them more mass and a larger structure.

Providing feedback to someone hurts. It's like rep number six on the third set—pain, burn, and shaking. We think of feedback as something harmful. Thus, referring to the cognitive reframing explained earlier, our thoughts create a belief system that causes us to either avoid or delay giving feedback. We, therefore, take no action, even though our gut tells us that we should, and we continue to get the same results we've been getting from those we lead.

If you want different results from people, you've got to start thinking about feedback in a different way. You've got to have the courage to confront people, to provide the feedback. Most likely, as you do so, it will hurt or tear them. Then, over time, and with the right nutrition (support), they will build back and become even stronger. If we embrace the thought that we are tearing so that we can build back stronger, then giving feedback becomes easier, and we become more motivated to do so. You can find a worksheet on building people up using the MUSCLE

> *Leadership is, among other things, the ability to inflict pain and get away with it ... short-term pain for long-term gain.*
> —George F. Will

method online at www.i2eyesquared.com/resources. This is such an important concept that I will come back to it in the chapter on collaboration.

In short, leaders that use the hammer to build recognize that sometimes you have to tear to build, and strive toward doing all they can to build the confidence of others. And, as you build the confidence of others, you gain more influence with them, thus increasing the degree of impact that you can have on their lives.

BECOMING A BUILDER

☐ **Reframe a Person.** Choose a person that you serve whom you don't have a high opinion of. How do you think about this person? How do your thoughts influence your beliefs about the person? What actions do you take based upon your beliefs and thoughts? What results are you getting from the person?

Thoughts: _____

Beliefs: _____

Actions: _____

Results: _____

What would it take to think about this person even a little bit differently? If you currently see the person as a four out of ten, look for evidence to help you see him or her as a five.

☐ **Kill Comparisons.** Comparison is a hope-killer! When we compare those we are speaking with to others, we decrease instead of increase hope. Stay away from comments such as "I wish you were more like…" and "If you could just do it like Susan can." The only person we should be compared to is ourselves. It is simply unreasonable to do otherwise, as no one has had the same experience, upbringing, education, or life circumstances.

☐ **Give an Opportunity.** Decide today to help boost others' self-confidence by giving them an opportunity. Find something that will highlight their natural strengths or skills. Let them know that this assignment may stretch them, and sometimes when we get stretched we fail. Let them know your belief in them and that if they do fail, you will be there to support them and help them learn through it.

☐ **Care to Confront.** Identify three people on your team right now. If you could speak freely and honestly, what would you tell them about their performance? Put a meeting in your calendar to sit with these three. Follow the MUSCLE method, where you tear down to build up.

Rule Number Three

CONNECT BEFORE YOU LEAD

He who thinks he leads, but has no followers, is only taking a walk.
—Ancient proverb

M ost don't realize this, but January of 2004 was a remarkable month. It was remarkable because this was when the masses of America first got to know Donald Trump, in a new reality television show *The Apprentice*. While what I write here is not intended to be interpreted into any sort of a political expression, I find a statement popularized by this show to be very alarming.

The premise of the show was to be the ultimate job interview in the ultimate jungle, with the winner being awarded a $250,000 salary to run one of Trump's businesses. Candidates who failed to perform were told "You're Fired!" and were asked to leave the show. This, however, is not the alarming statement that I'd like to bring attention to. It's the one that followed, one that encouraged fired candidates to not worry, because "It's not personal; it's just business."

The underlying meaning of this statement is that there does not need to be a connection between bosses and employees. That is, bosses have the title and authority and, hence, have no need to be connected to the followers: they can say or do anything without worry of offence, because "it's not personal; it's just business." This, my friends, is completely absurd. Leaders must connect to those they lead.

THE LOCOMOTIVE PRINCIPLE

I have four kids, and ever since my third child could peer out of the window from her car seat, she has been infatuated with trains. Even now, whenever she sees a train (which happens often in our small town), she yells out "trainee." She's eleven, and I keep telling her it is time to start calling them trains. Nonetheless, over the past decade, we've watched a lot of trains, and there is something basic that I've noticed through these years. There are two parts to a train: the locomotive and the boxcar. The locomotive houses all the power. It's the locomotive that has the ability to move, to pull, and to go.

A locomotive can transit from wherever you are reading this book to Chicago and back without a hiccup (unless you're reading this overseas, then there may be a slight issue in this analogy). However, if the locomotive arrives to Chicago and has no cargo (meaning that there are no boxcars behind it), then what is the point? Why travel to Chicago only to arrive there without any goods or cargo? You may say that it would be completely worthless, that there would be no point to it at all.

Sometimes, leaders are like this locomotive. They certainly have all the power to move, to pull, and to go, yet they often are "full steam ahead" without any boxcars. They move quickly down the pathway to success, only to arrive at a destination and recognize that they are alone, that they have not brought anyone or anything along. This is the type of leader that constantly complains that "it's lonely at the top." It's only lonely because they've not connected.

The locomotive principle says this: *a leader must connect to people to have value.* The real value of any organization is not the leader but, rather, the people. It's the people that get things done. It's the people that are doing the work. It's the people that make organizations function, and if you leave the people behind, you're neglecting the most valuable resource you have.

> **We are hardwired to connect with others, it's what gives our lives meaning and purpose.**
> –Brené Brown

Influential leaders have learned that if they are going at it alone, they are going to sink like a stone. These leaders recognize that to lead with influence, they must stop the locomotive, realign the tracks, and back up until the couplings of the locomotive and the couplings of the boxcar connect.

Allow me to add a very relevant side note here: The locomotive principle is especially pertinent in our age of technology. While the great benefits of technology have dramatically improved business, creating better efficiencies, and newer ways of doing things, it has also caused us to become less connected.

Emotional intelligence expert Daniel Goleman expresses that "today's children are growing up in a new reality, one where they are attuning more to machines and less to people than has ever been true in human history."[1]

I find it ironic that the very systems that have connected people across the world are the same systems that are creating a wide schism in personal connections in the workplace and at home. Too often, we would prefer to type out an email or send a text instead of picking up the phone or getting off our office chair to walk down the hallway.

Gradually, we are becoming more and more of a separated society; hence, there has never been a greater need for us as a people to become more connected, and I will help you understand how in this chapter.

PRODUCTIVITY OVER PEOPLE

For most of my experience in leadership, connecting with people has been my biggest weakness. Naturally, I am a very driven person. I love to-do lists. There is almost no greater satisfaction than finishing the day by crossing out everything on the little sticky note that I compose each morning. It makes me feel accomplished, like I've added value to the world, that I've used my time effectively.

As I've worked with leaders over the years, I've noticed that many are like me. Most leaders I've met are people that love to get things done, that set goals, and that meet their goals—people who evaluate their contribution to the world in terms of their productivity. In fact, I'd like to argue that a large part of how they got into leadership is this specific quality, that because they are so task-driven, they have been noticed and promoted. Perhaps this is the same for you.

Unfortunately, it is this very strength that has been the largest contributor to my weakness in connecting. You see, building relationships with people never made it onto my to-do list. How do you measure this? How do you determine if you've built a relationship? How can you evaluate what that relationship has done for the bottom line?

These are very difficult questions, so instead of working on them, I often ignored them and kept doing the things that I knew I could measure. To take this even further, I often saw people talking in the hallways or chatting about their personal lives, and I quickly judged them as time-wasters in my mind. I couldn't see the value of building connections and therefore placed no value on building relationships. Regrettably, this has led me to some very difficult places, including a specific portable classroom.

For me to become an influential leader, I had to work on this weakness. This is not to say that leaders of influence are leaders that ignore productivity or ones that diminish their drive for results. In the end, results matter, and there is no way to get around this. Rather, influential leaders are leaders who have the wisdom to understand that results go up when you take the time to connect with those you serve.

They realize that although connecting may seem "too soft" for business due to the lack of hard results, they must become intentional in their efforts to connect with people. The best leaders, those that have achieved great success, are leaders who place connecting with people high on their to-do list.

ROADBLOCKS TO CONNECTING

To connect, there are four common roadblocks that every person must move out of the pathway if they want to reach other people. Failure to honestly address these four roadblocks will inhibit or even remove your ability to connect with people.

An honest assessment will help you understand what you first need to work on to become a better connector. These four roadblocks are 1) Attitude, 2) Ego, 3) Insecurity, and 4) Fear.

Attitude

It's simple: if you don't want to connect with people, you won't. When it comes to connecting, there is no "faking it till you make it."

If you don't have a willing attitude to connect with people, they will see through you in less than thirty seconds and place more distance between you and them. Most leaders recognize the importance of having people buy into their vision. Some will then pretend to care, pretend to have concern for their people, in hopes that people will see their actions and then buy into their vision.

This is not how it works. You've probably heard the adage "People don't care how much you know until they know how much you care." What this means is that people must first feel your true emotion; they must feel that you want to connect before they open the doors and let you in. It all starts with a connecting attitude.

Ego

While attitude will get you in, you won't be able to stay long if you have a large ego. English Lord Acton stated, "Power tends to corrupt, and absolute power corrupts absolutely." A temptation for new leaders is to get a high sense of themselves once they get their title. It's as if their title suddenly makes them better than others. This feeling of being better than others is an ego, and leaders who have a large ego will never become leaders of influence.

> *Leadership is not a popularity contest; it's about leaving your ego at the door.*
> –Robin Sharma

The roadblock of ego was a difficult one for me. I was hired as a principal at the age of thirty-three. I had a graduate degree from one of the best schools in the Midwest, and I had risen through the ranks of education quickly. This gave me a sense of importance. Couple this with the fact that 80 percent of the people I was leading were older than me (some even double my age), and you can see why I developed an ego.

I'd like to say that I knew this was wrong from the beginning, but that would not be the truth. It felt good to think of myself as better than others. It felt good to have the title of principal. It felt good to be the most "powerful" person in the building. So, I'd stick out my chest and walk around the hallways like I was Teddy Roosevelt with his Big Stick. Looking back on it now, it is so clear why I couldn't connect with anyone. My ego was simply too large to fit through their door!

The opposite of ego is humility. Humility is a recognition that we don't have all the answers, that we can't do it alone, and that we do make mistakes. Spiritual leader Ezra Taft Benson explained that ego is a concern about *who* is right, while humility is being concerned about *what* is right. Once you've recognized that it is not about you being right and is instead about what is right, you'll be able to head further into the connecting door.

Insecurity

Let's say you're in a meeting with someone who has more experience than you do. You are their leader, and you feel like the conversation is going well . . . for the first few seconds. Suddenly, a feeling rushes through your mind that there's something wrong with you. Up until now, you were having a pretty good day. Abruptly, however, you've started to question who you are—everything from the accomplishments that you've achieved over your life, to your image, to the way that you talk.

You look at the person standing opposite you and start to envy them. You wish you had their hair, you wish you could speak like they do, that you had the respect that they command, or that you had the accomplishments that they have achieved. Suddenly, you feel inferior to them, and self-doubt floods your mind.

Consciously, you try to keep up your image, but subconsciously, your body is screaming to the other person that you are insecure about who you are. The subconscious of the other person is receiving and understanding the signals clearly and sends a message to their brain: "Something just doesn't feel right here. I'm not sure if I can trust or even follow this person. I think I'll stay closed with this one."

For you to connect with others, you've got to overcome your insecurities by first connecting with yourself. Do you know who you are? Do you know what you stand for? Do you fully appreciate your value? Are you comfortable enough with who you are that you don't worry about what others think about you?

> *When the leader lacks confidence, the followers lack commitment.*
> –John C. Maxwell

Taking the time to ponder questions like these will help you become more connected with yourself. Doing so will help you ignore the thoughts of insecurity or comparison with others and then revert your attention from yourself back to them.

Fear

Fear is universal. It affects every single one of us. Fear is the number-one thing that stops us from getting what we want in life. It's not ability, nor potential. It's not talent or skill. It's fear. Co-author of the *Chicken Soup for the Soul* series Jack Canfield says, "Everything you want is on the other side of fear."

Leaders want to connect with their people. They want to understand the strengths, the weaknesses, and the motivators of those they lead. The followers also want to connect. They want to know that they can trust their leader. They desire to understand expectations and vision and want to know that their leader is a normal human being. Unfortunately, fear is a major roadblock that stops us from getting these things, but how so?

First, it is often fear that stops us from taking the beginning step to connecting. Connectors understand that, although we are hardwired to connect, connecting doesn't naturally happen—you have to work at it. With this view, connectors recognize that they must be the ones to go first, to reach out, to approach a person, to start the conversation.

If you are like me, getting started is perhaps the scariest part of connecting, and, if left unaddressed, fear will stop us from being proactive and going first. Instead, we will sit back and wait for others to make connections with us. Beware: this is a follower mindset and not a leader mindset. Don't let yourself get into this fear trap.

The second issue is fearing that we are going to seem incompetent or just plain dumb. This fear causes us to put up a front, to add a few layers to our onion, to pretend to be something that we are not. We hold back who we really are and only express things that we believe will impress the other person. This fear can also cause us to simply say nothing or to be disengaged. We figure that if we say nothing, then there is nothing for the other person to judge and, therefore, we remain safe. Truly, fear is the great immobilizer. Unfortunately, relationships are not made by being fake, nor remaining silent.

We must recognize that, for the most part, fear is simply an imagination of the future. Daniel Goleman says fear is "the anxiety that has been unconscious and now pierces awareness."

Not long ago, I read that fear stands for False Evidence Appearing Real. It's our mind spinning through a thousand "What if's" and focusing on the negative ones, causing a spike in our heart rate, more sweat under our arms, and a resistance to do anything that might cause a negative "what if" to become a reality.

The best method for overcoming fear is simply to take action. Let your desire to make connections with people give you the courage to step through fear. When discussing fear, Nelson Mandela once said, "I learned that courage was not the absence of fear, but the triumph over it. The brave man is not he who does not feel afraid, but he who conquers that fear." To succeed on the other side, you must be brave and have the courage to make connections.

Now that we have identified and addressed each of these roadblocks, it's time for us to learn some specific steps for connecting with others. While a whole book could be written on this topic alone,

I'd like to share four of the most powerful connecting strategies that help to increase your degree of influence with others.

RIDICULOUSLY EXCEPTIONAL LISTENING

Think about people that have connected to you. What did they do? What caused you to open your coupling and allow a connection with the person? Most likely, in some form, your answer to these questions is that they made you feel like you matter. The best way to help people feel like they matter is to become a Ridiculously Exceptional Listener (REL).

Now, you may think that you are already a great listener and that it is the others who needs to improve their listening skills. If this is true, then you can probably relate to a man named Harold.

Harold was certain that his wife had a hearing problem, and as any good spouse does, he was looking for an opportunity to prove it. Finally, one day, he noticed his wife in the far corner of the living room, with her back turned toward him.

He, in a regular voice, said, "Honey, can you hear me?"

His wife didn't respond.

He took a few steps closer and repeated, "Honey, can you hear me?" Still, nothing.

Again, he moved closer and said, "Honey, can you hear me?" with the same lack of response.

Finally, right next to her, he asked, "Honey, can you hear me?"

His wife turned around, looked at him and said, "Harold, for the fourth time, I can hear you!"

It was Harold that had the hearing problem, not his wife.

Unfortunately, Ridiculously Exceptional Listeners are very rare. Take a moment and ponder—how many really good, active listeners do you know? I've asked this question to numerous audiences, and the results are always the same. Few can name more than five, most can only name two or three, and the rest can only name one.

Ivan Misner, founder of the networking organization Business Network International, often says that the average person knows about 250 people. Out of all those that we know, most of us can only name two or three exceptional listeners—that's just ridiculous!

While listening is the number-one way to connect with others, when we look at the work done by the American Institutes of Research, it makes sense why most people are bad listeners.[2] This research states that our brain processes about 450 words per minute. Yet, even a fast-talking New Yorker only averages about a hundred fifty words per minute. This means that it takes just 25 percent of our brain power to listen to someone speak. No wonder we often get distracted while we're supposed to be listening to someone, by thinking instead about our to-do lists, our favorite TV show, or what we are going to do when we get home from work.

You can relate this to driving a car. Have you ever come home, entered your driveway, and thought, "Hum, how did I get here?" You can do this because you can drive on auto-pilot. You have more brain power than is necessary to drive. The same goes for listening, you can be on auto-pilot because listening to the words only does not take much brain power.

Since it does not take all our brain power to listen, we often start listening on autopilot. This may be okay, unless the person speaking stops and asks you a question or if you're trying to establish a connection. Then our auto-drive gets us into trouble.

RELs are people who have overcome the temptation to use the remaining 75 percent of their brain power for things other than listening. They have found strategies and uses for their brains that not only allow them to communicate "you

> *Listening, not imitation, may be the sincerest form of flattery.*
> —Joyce Brothers

matter," but also to connect much better and more quickly that most people. RELs recognize at least seven benefits of active listening:

- It provides a good impression to the person speaking.
- It communicates "You matter" to the speaker.
- It shows the other person that you value his or her opinion.
- It's a great way to learn new information.
- It creates trust.
- It provides clarity, thus reducing conflict and confusion.
- It decreases mistakes.

BECOMING AN REL

If you are interested in one or more of these benefits to active listening, you are in luck. Listening is a skill, and because it is a skill, you can study it, learn it, and become better at it.

Below, you can find five practical methods for improving your ability to listen and, therefore, your ability to connect. Although some of these five methods may not seem new, don't overlook the power that each one holds in connecting with others.

1. Admit You've Got a Problem

A casual observer of any addiction-recovery program will recognize that the first step to getting better is frankly admitting the problem. To be a better listener, you must recognize that you can become better. This means having the humility and the desire to improve your listening skills. If you don't first have a desire, your efforts to connect with others will be greatly limited.

2. Remove the Distractions

In 2015, the management consulting company Accenture conducted a survey of 3,600 working professionals from thirty different countries, ranging from entry-level to management, across generations and genders. Their findings are remarkable. Their data states that while nearly all (96 percent) of the respondents consider themselves good listeners, two-thirds admit that listening is becoming much more difficult due to the distractions.[3] Our habitual efforts to multi-task while speaking has significantly reduced our ability to be an REL.

Try people-watching in any crowded area, and you'll notice many in conversation with friends who also are looking things up, cruising Facebook, or texting on their phones. We have this idea that we can multitask, that since our brains can take in all that is being said and do much more, we should be doing much more. Unfortunately, this is not true.

Earl Miller, a professor of neuroscience at MIT, states that "People can't multitask very well, and when people say they can, they're deluding themselves. The brain is very good at deluding itself." Simply put, we can't focus on more than one thing at a time. Therefore, the old myth that we can multitask is just that: a myth, and science now proves it.

As we make efforts to remove the distractions that surround us when we engage in conversation, we will hear more. It's like the poem about a wise, old owl:

> A wise, old owl sat on an oak.
> The more he saw, the less he spoke;
> the less he spoke, the more he heard.
> Why aren't we like that wise, old bird?

This is not something that I've always been good at. I recall one teacher who was a constant complainer. You know the type: they complain about their work duties, complain about the people they must work with, complain about their work environment, and, yes, even complain that their tomatoes didn't ripen in 1984.

Since I was still believing the multitasking myth, honestly, I didn't care about this person's complaints. Whenever she would come by my office, I would continue my multitasking. For example, when she entered with a complaint, if I were in the middle of an email, I would simply turn my head, acknowledge her presence, and pretend to listen to her, all the while continuing to type out my email. Yes, I was really this bad!

> *Leaders who don't listen will eventually be surrounded by people who have nothing to say.*
> —Andy Stanley

One day, after reflecting on my inability to connect, I decided to pick up the toothbrush with the other hand—I decided to try to listen differently. The very morning that I made this decision, guess who was the first person into my office? Yup, Mrs. Constant Complainer.

I had made a resolution, so I was going to change my habits, even if it was with someone I didn't like. As she entered, I pushed aside my keyboard, turned my monitor, squared my shoulders with hers, looked into her eyes, and asked, "How can I help you?"

For the next three minutes, she went on one of her typical rants. At the conclusion, I said, "Thank you for letting me know. I appreciate it and will see what I can do." I felt good—I was actually starting to be a better listener—but that wasn't even the best thing about our experience.

After leaving my office, she went upstairs toward her classroom. She gathered together all her teacher buddies, then told them how wonderful of a listener I was and that I really cared. In only three minutes of active listening, I started to change the entire culture of our building.

To be a better listener, don't pick up your cell phone (even if it vibrates); move yourself away from the computer screen; refrain from looking at your smartwatch; get away from other people, machines, or areas that may distract you from the person speaking; and focus on what the person is saying. You'll find that removing distractions will be a wise investment.

3. Restrain Judgment

Our brains are the most amazing supercomputers. They are constantly processing information from all our senses and determining what to do with this information. This is currently, and has always been, critical to our survival. Imagine what would have happened if our ancient ancestors saw a tiger and did not make the lightning-fast judgment to run or defend. Yet, in our modern day, when it comes to listening, there is value in fighting this natural, age-old tendency.

Too often, as we listen to others, we get caught up in judgments. What are they saying? Does this agree with my beliefs? Why are they talking that way? Can't they tell I'm done listening? What are they wearing? Why would they wear that? Is he really telling the truth or just trying to make himself look good?

While these questions are not necessarily bad, if we are constantly asking ourselves questions as others are speaking, we will miss out on much of what they are trying to say and will formulate inaccurate conclusions that are not based upon all the facts.

The best RELs clear their minds of judgments while the other person is talking. They simply listen, ask additional questions if necessary, and then make their judgments.

4. Be Okay with Pauses

Think about the last conversation that you had with someone whom you didn't know too well. Most likely, there was a point in the conversation when both of you stopped talking. How comfortable was that for you?

I have found in my work with people that we will do almost anything to avoid that uncomfortable pause. For us Minnesotans, that means we will bring up the weather. It's always changing, and therefore, there is always something to talk about. I've seen such conversations extend well beyond ten minutes, discussing weather patterns, comparing this winter with the last one, and even bringing up such things as the record-breaking Halloween winter storm of 1991, all to avoid the uncomfortable pause in conversation. We humans fear running out of things to say.

Due to this fear, in most of our conversations, we are listening, but we are thinking about what we are going to say next more. Unfortunately, thinking about what to say next distracts us from what is being said and causes us to be bad listeners.

Not to sound like a broken record, but if we can remove the temptation to conjure up our next statement while the other is talking, and, instead, keep a clear mind, then we will become better listeners. In fact, there are two great benefits to allowing pause.

First, because we were able to listen better while the other was talking, our response—be it a question or a comment—will be richer and more valuable to the conversation. Second, believe it or not, the person will actually have a greater degree of respect for you, because you have taken the efforts necessary to truly understand what is being said. Both benefits should outweigh our fear of the pause.

5. Pay Ridiculous Attention

Of course, Ridiculously Exceptional Listeners would not be exceptional if they did not pay a ridiculous amount of attention. Remember all that extra brain power that we have? We can put that to use by paying ridiculous attention to what is being said.

Two French neuroscientists of the 1980s, Bandler and Grinder, provided some amazing research on what we can focus the extra brain power on. According to their research, all people favor a certain sensory experience in their communication, a certain way that they think about communicating, and a certain way that they use words when they communicate.[4] This is called a sensory preference.

Let's say that you love to see things in pictures, that when you are trying to explain an idea, you visualize it in your mind first. Because of this, expressing your thoughts and ideas is something you can do quickly and easily. If this describes you, most likely your sensory preference is visual.

Now imagine you're hanging out with a friend who is describing an idea but is not using too many visual words. He is expressing how certain things make him feel. He's taking a long time to fully explain himself, and it's driving you nuts. You want to say, "Hurry up and just spit it out, will you?"

Of course, you don't, because that would be rude. Plus, you're reading this book, and you really are trying to listen better, but you're wondering if you have the patience.

Instead of jumping to the conclusion that this person is merely slow or that he doesn't know how to express himself, you may calm your frustration by learning that his sensory preference is different than yours. That is, he interprets and expresses himself with a different sensory method: in this case, kinesthetic.

Research from Bandler and Grinder suggests that all of us—every human being—fall into having one of three sensory preferences: visual, auditory, and kinesthetic.

Generally speaking, people that are visuals see things in pictures. They speak at a higher tone and a faster pace, because it is easy to describe a picture. You can recognize these individuals when you hear statements such as "I see what you are saying," "Fascinating perspective," "Let me show you," or "Can you imagine?"

As you've noticed, the words they choose tend to align with their preferred sensory mode because they use vision-based words ("see," "perspective," "show," "imagine"). When visuals are developing a new idea or trying to recall an experience, they tend to look up as if trying to see a picture in the sky.

Auditories are individuals that are all about the sound of things. They often have great voices, perfect tone, and wonderful pitch. Think Ed Sheeran or Matthew McConaughey. You'll find auditories using phrases such as "Sounds familiar," "He's outspoken," "I didn't like her tone of voice," and "Hey, listen." Audies will look side to side, toward their ears, when trying to be creative or recall information.

Kinesthetics, or Kinos, prefer to interpret and express things through feeling. This can be the actual feel of physical touch or the feelings of the heart. They tend to speak the slowest and have a deeper voice, because it is much harder to express a feeling than a picture. You'll recognize them when they use phrases such as "How do you feel about that?", "He's a pain in the neck," or "I'm under a lot of stress." Interestingly, Kinos will tend to look down, or toward their heart, when thinking.

> *A house full of people is a house full of different points of view.*
> –Maori Proverb

Now, my intention in explaining these basic principles of sensory preferences is not to promote you to expert in identifying the preferences of others. No, rather, I mention this to prove a point. I state this to show that there is so much more that we can be focusing on during conversation. There is so much more we can be using our brains for.

How fast are people speaking? What is happening to the tone of their voice? What seem to be their favorite words (the words they use over and over again)? Put your mind to use by paying ridiculous attention to what is being said and how it is being said.

IT'S NOT JUST THE WORDS

If you've started to focus on the "what" and "how" of listening, then you are ready for the next component of connecting. Again, I turn to some compelling research to help us understand this second component.

Communications expert and UCLA professor emeritus Albert Mehrabian has done extensive work on determining what really conveys the meaning of our message: when we are trying to get a point across to someone, what parts of our speech are the most powerful, and which are the least powerful?

His findings are revealing. Mehrabian has uncovered that what we say (the words) accounts for only 7 percent of our meaning, while 38 percent of our meaning is based upon the way we say it (tone), and a whopping 55 percent is based upon our body language (the nonverbal behavior).

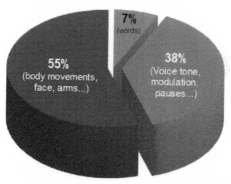

Most likely, in your experiences on the other side, you've already had to give a presentation of some sort. Most often, presentations from leaders are given to cause action or to change how a group thinks about something. I wonder, how much time did you spend on the actual words you were going to say?

If you are like most, almost all your preparation time went into the exact words you were going to use. In fact, you may have been so nervous about it that you scripted the presentation out, word-for-word, and recited it multiple times.

All these preparation steps are wonderful, and you should do them. However, based upon the research from Mehrabian, if you really want to connect, then you need to take your preparation a step further and ensure proper practice of tone and body language—for here is where the real meaning will come from.

This is clearly evident in presentations where the body language does not match what's being said. Several years ago, I was sitting in an important meeting with twenty-five other school administrators. The superintendent of this relatively large school district was giving a presentation about new software that was intended to help us map out the career pathways of our students, beginning in eighth grade.

Since this was going to dramatically change our job responsibilities, you could tell he'd taken great amounts of time to craft the perfect speech. It was articulate, complete with a statement of the problem, reasons why this was the best solution, stories about how this could impact students, and how there would be support for us to make the change: all the necessary elements of a persuasive speech.

Yet, as we walked out of this meeting, my colleagues and I started talking about how something didn't feel right. We couldn't exactly pinpoint it, but it seemed like he wasn't behind this change. We all had the same feeling that he was doing this because someone else (perhaps the school board) was putting him up to it. Needless to say, the implementation of this software was more or less a flop.

> *The single biggest problem in communication is the illusion that it has taken place.*
> —George Bernard Shaw

If I had a video recording of this event, most likely what I would find is that his words and his body language did not match. Even though I didn't have the awareness of nonverbal communication that I do now, my subconscious picked up on this discrepancy and caused me not to be influenced by his well-crafted speech.

As a leader who connects, it is critical to watch for these moments of variance between what is being said and how it is being said, both in your personal communication and the communication of others. Let's look at a couple of examples.

Say you've got a new idea that would streamline a process that one of your direct-reports runs. You are excited about this idea, and since it affects your direct report, you call her in. You sit across the desk from her as you explain your new brilliant idea. She seems interested, because she keeps saying things like "Wow, that is a great idea!" and "Yeah, I think we could make this work," but something feels off.

You observe her actions a little more closely and recognize that she is using a "blocking" behavior. This is when someone is uncomfortable with an idea, and they try to block themselves off from others, such as when people bring their hand down their face and over their eyes. With her, you've noticed that she is using the report that she had in her hand to block portions of her upper body or even parts of her face. It's like she wants to hide, but her words are saying that this is a good idea.

A person whose attention is not fully committed to the conversation would probably miss this subtle sign. However, not you. Since you've noticed the gap between her words and her nonverbals, you stop and ask some follow-up questions. "I'm glad you are taking this so well." Say, "Usually, when I ask others to change the way they do things, they feel a little scared at first. It's like they have some concerns, but they don't want to upset anyone, so they simply don't mention them. Could this be how you feel?"

A question like this could open a deep concern and, therefore, help you and the person you serve become more connected.

Other common nonverbals include beating, pacifying, and leaning. I encourage you to seek out more learning in this area. In the meantime, allow me to share a few more basics.

If you are presenting the same idea and notice that your direct report is bouncing her leg up and down, almost to a beat, then this is a good sign. You've got the person's interest and support—you're building a connection.

If you are presenting the idea and find yourself constantly rubbing your hands together, rubbing your neck, or rubbing the top of your legs, you could be in for some trouble. It's like you're pacifying a crying baby by rubbing its back, except you are the baby. You are subconsciously telling your direct-reporter that you are nervous about this conversation, and the person may assume that your nervousness equates a lack of confidence in the idea.

> **The most important thing in communication is hearing what isn't said.**
> –Peter Drucker

Perhaps you are standing with a direct-report who is giving you some critical feedback and you begin leaning backward like you're wanting to run from the situation.

The other person observes this (most likely subconsciously) and determines that you really don't care, even though you thank the person for having the courage to speak up. When people lean back, they are uncomfortable and want to exit the conversation. When they lean in, they are engaged and excited about what is being said, which is a sign that they want to connect with you.

Again, the purpose of this book is not to make you an expert on body language. However, I am trying to help you become a better connector. Making the decision to be a better listener is an important starting point and using all your brain power to be attuned to tone and body language brings you far down the road to genuine connection. Failure to do either of these almost guarantees that no connection will be made. Great connectors understand that connecting is about the words AND the other communicators of the message.

The Chameleon Effect

Before I move away from the topics of words, tone, and body language, let me explain one more benefit of paying ridiculous attention to this trio. By careful observation during communication, you'll be able to more accurately identify when you've connected with the other person.

When you've connected, a rapport is established with that person. This is the golden ticket for connecting with people. A rapport is a close and harmonious relationship with another person, where you both understand each other's feelings or ideas and where you both communicate smoothly. Establish a rapport, and you'll establish influence. But how do you know if you've really got it? How do you know if the feelings in your gut are true feelings of a connection?

To answer this question, we turn to a groundbreaking report from two Yale scientists. Published in 1999, this report disclosed to the world the idea of the Chameleon Effect. This term describes the subconscious actions that we take to match or mirror others with whom we have established rapport.

To match means to copy the words, tone, and body language of another. To mirror means to provide a mirror image of the person. For instance, if the person you are speaking with has the right hand on his or her chin, and you do too, this is matching. If one of you is copying the other's actions but with the other hand, then you are mirroring.

The Chameleon Effect begins when we are babies as we match and mirror our mother. It is in great effect during our teenage years where we copy how our friends talk and act. This continues throughout our life in the most intimate relationships we develop.

A perfect example of this comes from an experience that I had as a pastor of a church. As the leader, I sat with my two counselors on the stand in front of the entire congregation. One Sunday, after services, my wife told me that she noticed something interesting during our meeting. She said that I had my hands clasped between my legs but moved them so that one arm crossed my chest while the other arm was raised up at ninety degrees to support my head.

Then, less than twenty seconds later, the guy on my right did the same thing, and just a few seconds after that, the guy on my left followed. Suddenly, all three of us had an arm across our chest with the other supporting our chin. This example of the Chameleon Effect makes great sense, as I have a deep rapport with both men, having spent years in service with them.

A few Sundays later, during an especially boring sermon, I wanted to have a little fun by putting this effect to the true test. I intentionally brought one leg up and placed it upon the other in a crossed position. Sure enough, my two counselors followed suit.

Paying ridiculous attention to words, tone, and body language can not only help you become a better communicator, but it is also key to identifying if you've established a rapport with the person by watching for the Chameleon Effect.

COMMON GROUND CONNECTS

The third strategy to connecting is finding common ground. To celebrate our fifteenth year of marriage, my wife and I took a trip to the island of St. Kitts in the Caribbean. Being a natural introvert, I love the island life. There is little I look forward to more than setting up a lounge chair at the beach on a hot and sunny day. I always bring along a book with me, and I enjoy the solitude of getting away from everyone and everything as I fall into reading.

My wife Sarah, however, is not an introvert. She has an uncanny ability of striking up a conversation with just about any stranger. Therefore, it was not much of a surprise when, while deep into my reading, I heard her say, "That's a nice hat."

I slowly peered over my book and noticed that she has struck up a conversation with someone that could not be more opposite than me. He was short, a little chubby, African-American, had dreadlocks, and you could tell that he was an artsy sort of person. I smiled gently and then sank back into my book, knowing that Sarah is used to my introverted behavior and wouldn't mind. Honestly, due to the apparent contrasts between him and me, I really had no interest in getting to know this person.

A few minutes of conversation had passed, when his response to one of Sarah's questions caused me to sit up, close my book, and engage in conversation.

The question was innocent enough: "Where are you from?"

It was the answer that caused a change in my behavior.

"St. Paul, Minnesota."

Instantly, we—two people who appeared to be from very different worlds—were connected 2,500 miles away from what we both call home.

Why? What caused me and this stranger to instantly become connected? It's quite simple really: we found something that we both could relate to. We found common ground.

Great connectors are avid seekers of common ground. They understand that this is the keystone to the arch, the dama to the quinceanera, the fish to the fish tank. Finding common ground really is the whole point to all our listening and observation, and it provides the glue that will make connections stick.

This can be found around something personal (such as fishing, the gym, or cars), or it can be something professional (such as what motivates you, what your career aspirations are, or what college you attended). Either way, when you've found common ground, you've now established a connection, and you can start to move that locomotive forward.

Discovering the commonalities between me and the other guy has been pretty challenging. While I love to dive deep on a topic with someone, I really don't like the efforts that are necessary to go from "I don't know you" to "We have this in common." Often, this involves small talk, and I'm not naturally good at this. However, wanting to build a business and understanding the importance for leaders to connect with people, I've learned an easy but powerful secret to finding common ground with others.

The Secret to Common Ground

Let's say you've got an employee that you'd really like to connect with. You know that the person could perform better, but you recognize that if you just started with a blunt, open expression of your thoughts, then you'll probably sever the relatively weak relationship you have with this person.

Furthermore, you understand that if you stated your mind without connecting, you'd be leading more from your title than from influence. You've made it far enough in this book to understand that this could be a terrible mistake. What can you do to find common ground and form a stronger connection so that you can truly help this person recognize more of his or her potential? The secret is to ask questions.

Think back to Sarah and the gentleman she sat next to at St. Lucas. How were we able to find common ground? It was through her questions that she discovered what we had in common.

Not only do questions help us discover more about the other person, but it also shows the other person that we care and that we are interested in what is being said. Besides, what's our number-one most favorite topic to talk about? Ourselves, of course, and by asking questions of your conversation partners, you are asking them to talk more about themselves.

> *The art and science of asking questions is the source of all knowledge.*
> –Thomas Berger

Allow me to share a couple of strategies that have helped me find common ground through questions. The first is FORM. FORM stands for Family, Organization, Recreation and Mission.

Whenever I first start a conversation with someone, I will often revert to one of these four topics and create a question around it.

Here are a few examples:

- "Do you have family that live in the area?" (Family)
- "Tell me, how long have you been working at X company?" (Organization)

- "What has been the biggest change that you've seen in the last five years in your industry/our company?" (Organization)
- "What do you enjoy doing in your free time?" (Recreation)
- "How did you spend your weekend?" (Recreation)
- "What drives you to work hard?" (Mission)

You'll notice that most of these are soft, and that is a great way to start a conversation, especially if you don't know the person too well. However, I strongly encourage you to dig deeper as soon as possible. You see, it's one thing to have fishing in common. This connects people, and it can give you something to talk about. Yet, it's a whole different thing to connect on more personal and emotionally-filled ideas. To get deeper, I tend to use another strategy that I call the Three Key Questions. It may seem weird that I have strategies for questions, but remember, I'm an introvert, and I have to plan my questions so I can feel comfortable in conversations.

The three Key Questions are these:

"What do you dream about?"
"What do you sing about?"
"What do you cry about?"

The dream is the vision, the goal, the big idea that people would like to achieve in life. This is what inspires them to get up in the morning. It's their vision of how they see themselves in ten years. It's how they would like to be remembered at their funeral.

When you ask about singing, you are asking about the good things that are happening in life right now. That is, what is going on right now that they are super excited about. These are things that they will post on social media or will write about in their annual Christmas letter.

We cry over issues that bother us, so this question is asking others about things that keep them up at night, things that they really worry about or stress about. It's the failures, the shortcomings, the challenges in life that they are not sure they can handle.

I call these the Three Key Questions, because if you can find a person's answers to these questions, you have unlocked and opened the door to a deep connection. You can either ask the question as it is directly written here or modify it.

"If you had $100,000 to spend, what would you spend it on?" is a question you could use to get insight into their dream.

"If you had a genie in a bottle that could remove any challenge in your life, what would you remove?" is an example of a modified "What do you cry about?" question.

Exceptional connectors make it their goal to find common ground on a deep level. They look for similarities in values, in morals, in their beliefs about the world, people, and the business. Go back to the character example of Gandhi. People connected with Gandhi and his belief in nonviolent resistance. Millions not only agreed with him but were also willing to put their lives at risk to stay connected to him and this idea.

Imagine the sort of connection that you can make with the employee who has more potential when you learn that both of you have a passion for helping at-risk kids. Of course, you'd never get there unless you continued to ask questions. Truly, the secret to common ground is asking questions.

BE SIGNIFICANT IN SERVICE

There is no doubt that leaders who listen, pay attention to body language, and use questions to find common ground are leaders who connect to those they serve.

However, there is one additional strategy that, if applied, is sure to close the gap between the locomotive and the boxcar. You may not have picked up on it yet, but if you go back through this book, you'll notice that almost every time that I refer to those you lead, I don't use words such as "subordinate," "minion," or "follower." Rather, I use the phrase "those you serve."

This is an intentional choice in wording, as the best leaders are leaders who, at their core, have a desire to serve others. These leaders agree with physician and missionary Sir Wilfred T. Grenfell, who said, "The service we render to others is really the rent we pay for our room on this earth."

Influential leader President Woodrow Wilson expressed that we are here "not merely to make a living" but instead to "enable the world to live more amply, with greater vision, with a finer spirit of home and achievement." He added that we are here "to enrich the world, and you impoverish yourself if you forget the errand."

It's a wonderful fact of life, that as we serve others, we create a special bond, or connection, with those we serve. We grow closer in our relationships when we take the time to serve others. Certainly, "Our success in life is directly related to the quality and quantity of our service to others," as Earl Nightingale stated.

But how do we make our service significant? Service occurs when a person goes above and beyond to provide help, assistance, or encouragement to another. When someone listens or observes close enough to identify a special need and then takes the actions to assist with that need, the service then becomes significant. That is, this type of service leaves a memorable impression upon us, it resonates in our minds, it makes an impact that we don't easily forget: it becomes significant. And significant service leads to a significant connection.

Here is a simple example. I was cold-calling to an electrical contracting company. As is typical, the person I wanted to speak with was "busy." I got a business card and started to walk out of the building when I noticed a woman struggling in the parking lot. She was trying to carry more cleaning products than her hands would allow. I quickly went over, grabbed a few things for her, and brought them into the business's building, then I left.

A few days later, I phoned the business. The receptionist picked up the phone and, once she realized who I was, immediately transferred me to the person I wanted. I didn't even serve the receptionist, yet she saw the service, and it made a significant enough impact upon her that she bypassed the typical company policy of not letting cold calls through, which got me connected to the right person.

The idea of giving significant service is to become remarkable in your actions for others. You have honest intent to help another, discover what would be beneficial for the person, and take the action necessary. Consequently, you leave a memorable or significant impact on the individual. Here is a heart-warming story that provides another prime example of significant service:

> A man and a teenage boy checked into a hotel and were shown to their room. The hotel staff noted the quiet manner of the guests and the pale appearance of the boy. After a few minutes in their room, the man and boy came out to eat dinner in the hotel's restaurant. Again, the staff noticed the two and thought that something was off. Both the boy and his father were silent, neither looked too interested in their food, and their faces expressed a deep degree of somberness. When they completed their dinner, the boy went back to their room, while the man approached the front desk.
>
> "May I see the manager, please?"
>
> Concerned, the receptionist replied, "Is everything okay? Are you satisfied with your room? Is there something that we can fix?"
>
> "Thanks," replied the man, "everything with our room is fine, but I would still like to see the manager."
>
> The manager came out and asked that the man join him in the privacy of his office. The boy's father then began to explain that he was spending the night with his fourteen-year-old-son, who was seriously ill, probably terminally so. The boy

was to undergo therapy the next day, which would cause him to lose his hair. They had come to spend one night together before embarking on the battle of this illness. On this night, they were going to shave their heads as a symbolic gesture that the two of them were going to win this fight.

He stated, "The reason that I asked for your time is that I really don't want any strange looks. My son has been very sensitive about this, and I just wanted to let you know so that you could let your staff know and therefore avoid anything that might be uncomfortable."

That night, they both shaved their heads. The next morning, the man and his son, with a little more energy for life, left their hotel room and sat down for breakfast. As they pondered what to eat, they noticed something significant. To their great surprise, each of the four staff members on duty for breakfast had shaved heads.

These individuals recognized the tremendous need for this young boy to feel supported in his trials. This is the kind of service that is significant. This is the sort of service that truly shows others that you care. This is the service that connects. When we make this kind of connection, the miraculous thing is that not only does it become significant to the person we served, but the joy of doing so also becomes significant to us.

If you think that you can lead by ignoring others; by pushing forward your own agenda; or by ignoring the interests, desires, and needs of others, then you are gravely mistaken. This is not leadership. Leaders of influence are connectors because they care enough to listen, pay ridiculous attention, find common ground, and are always striving to give significant service.

> *Only a life lived for others is a life worthwhile.*
> –Albert Einstein

CONNECTING WITH YOUR BOXCARS

☐ **Take the Listening Test.**

1. Do I wait until the other person is done speaking before I respond?
2. Do I suspend my judgment until after the conversation?
3. Do I ask questions to clarify?
4. Do I respond to emails and texts while talking on the phone?
5. Do I repeat what I've heard back to the speaker before asserting my point?
6. As I listen, do I keep my body language engaged by facing the person, making eye contact, and nodding when appropriate?
7. Do I daydream while listening to people express their thoughts?
8. In a conversation, do I talk less than the other person?
9. Do I frequently interrupt the other person?
10. Do I acknowledge that I can always be a better listener?

☐ **"T" Up Your Time.** Connecting with people takes time. Print off a blank day calendar with fifteen-minute increments. Draw a large "T" down the page, and write "connecting" on one side and "doing" on the other. Every fifteen minutes put a checkmark on the correct column based upon where you spent your time. Find a template for this at www.i2eyesquared.com/resources.

☐ **Have a Connecting Conversation.** Purposely schedule a fifteen-minute conversation with someone you need to connect with. Practice each of the principles in this chapter during the conversation, then take the Connecting Assessment located at www.i2eyesquared.com/resources.

☐ **Use the Three Key Questions.** Write down the names of four people you'd like to connect with. Complete the following questions for all four. Strive to fill in any gaps.

Name:

- What do they dream about?
- What do they sing about?
- What do they cry about?

Rule Number Four

COLLABORATE TO BE GREAT

If everyone is moving forward together, then success takes care of itself.

—Henry Ford

There's an old story about an anthropologist who had been studying the culture and habits of a South African tribe. He had been working in that village for some time, and on the last day of his stay, he proposed a game to the children of the village.

He prepared a big basket full of fruit and treats from the region and placed it under a tree. He marked a line on the earth a hundred feet away and instructed the children to run at the count of three. Whoever reached the basket first would be entitled to the whole basket for themselves.

So, the kids did as instructed, but the result greatly surprised the anthropologist. Instead of all the kids running as fast as they could for the prize, they ran together, holding hands, toward the basket. When they reached it, they all shared what was in it.

Later, the anthropologist asked the children, "Why did you all run together when one of you could have gotten the whole basket?"

A young little girl replied, "How can one of us be happy if all the others aren't?"

This simple story is an example of an African philosophy called *Ubuntu. Ubuntu,* loosely translated, means "I am, because we are." Nelson Mandela expounded upon this when he stated that Ubuntu is "the profound sense that we are human only through the humanity of others, that if we are to accomplish anything in this world, it will in equal measure be due to the work and achievements of others."

YOU CAN'T DO IT ALONE

I believe that we Americans have a lot to learn from our friends in South Africa. Ours is a highly individualistic and competitive society, beginning with a four-year-old in Little League soccer and stretching all the way into our senior years. We honor and celebrate the accomplishments of the individual through our movies, our books, and our halls of fame. Rarely do we acknowledge the work of a team, but almost always, we idolize and aspire to be like the successful individual.

> Great things in business are never done by one person.
> –Steve Jobs

Unfortunately, many leaders embrace the Lone Ranger myth. We think that our success, our accomplishments, and the contribution that we can make to society is strictly based upon our individual efforts. We therefore trudge through our challenges, pull ourselves up by the bootstraps when we fall, and push forward to make a difference in this world as individuals.

However, the real truth is this: nothing of significance has ever been accomplished by an individual acting alone.

Bill Gates had Paul Allen, Mark Zuckerberg had Eduardo Saverin and Dustin Moskowitz, Isaac Newton had Edmund Halley, Charles

Lindbergh had a team of businessmen, and even the Lone Ranger had Tonto.

I think former MIT dean Lester C. Thurow said it best when he said this:

> There is nothing antithetical in American history, culture, or traditions to teamwork. Teams were important in America's history... wagon trains conquered the West; men working together on an assembly line conquered the world; successful national strategy and a lot of teamwork put an American on the moon... but American mythology extols only the individual... In America, halls of fame exist for almost every conceivable activity, but nowhere do Americans raise monuments in praise of teamwork.

Try as you might on your own, but you will quickly realize that if you want to see growth, if you want to see improvement, if you want to see better results in your organization, then you have to work through a team. And that requires that you co-labor, or collaborate, with others. Quite simply, you can't get it done with just one!

THE TEAMSTER PRINCIPLE

A few years ago, in a small midwestern town, people gathered to watch a highly competitive annual horse pull. This year's event was especially exciting because there were two individuals who had strong horses, and both were determined to win this pull.

The contest proved to meet all the anticipated expectations, as each man and beast pulled an incredible amount of weight. Through fierce competition, one man became victor by pulling 4,300 pounds, and the other had to face defeat, losing by just 200 pounds.

Despite the rivalry during the day, the two began talking around evening. After a drink or two, they became best buddies, and a creative idea struck them. What would happen if they tied both the horses together to pull the sled? How much would the horses be able to pull? They followed this idea to reality and were greatly shocked when the two of them pulled not the expected combined weight of 8,400 pounds, but 12,000 pounds, an increase of 30 percent!

Had these two done their homework, they would have known that this should be no surprise at all. In fact, from colonial times to the turn of the twentieth century, men who drove horse-drawn wagons have capitalized on this principle. For decades, teamsters (a term used to describe those who led the wagons) formed the backbone of North America's wealth and prosperity by tying horses together and transporting goods all across the continent.

> *Alone, we can do so little. Together, we can do so much.*
> –Helen Keller

The life of a teamster was tough. Often, they would work twelve to eighteen hours a day, seven days a week, for an average of two dollars per day (which is about fifty dollars a day in 2018). Despite how we picture it in our minds, teamsters often did not sit in the wagon; rather, they walked along with their horses, encouraging them and making the adjustments to ensure that the load arrived intact and on time—for if they didn't, it was the teamster that had to pay.

This required them to work very closely with the horses, yoking or connecting them as a team, ensuring that each was pulling to its fullest capacity, and redirecting them so that each one of them was constantly aligned in the direction of the destination. It was because of these harsh conditions that they organized and formed one of America's first and largest unions by the same name.

Although their jobs were difficult, they were clear on two things. First, results matter. If they did not get the cargo delivered, they did not get paid. Their entire livelihood depended upon getting results. Second, you can pull a much heavier load and have better results with multiple horses working together than you can with one horse.

You've probably already started to make some correlations between the work of the teamster and the responsibilities of a leader. Teamsters and leaders do a lot of the same things. They both have a goal in mind, they both have to get results, they both work with a team, and they both can't get it done unless that team collaborates with each other. This is why I've chosen the teamster to represent collaboration. Simply put, the teamster principle says this: *Extraordinary results happen when we're all pulling together.*

Most likely, you've noticed that from your very first working day, results matter. Perhaps you started out as a babysitter or a mower of lawns. You had to ensure that you took care of the kids or mowed the lawns nicely if you wanted to be paid. As you've progressed in your working career, each progression was probably due to your ability to get things done. Now that you are on the other side, getting results is even more important. The ability to remain and progress as a leader is directly related to your ability to get results. Just like the teamster, to get results, you must get others to work together, to collaborate. There is nothing that speaks more about your skill as a leader than the results that you can produce through others.

COLLABORATION

This rule of leadership is different than the previous three. The first rule, Character Counts, is all about who you are and how your example becomes the model for others to follow. Building the Confidence of Others, the second rule, provides motivation to those you encounter each day. As you strive to Connect Before You Lead, the third rule, you begin to receive permission to have a deeper impact on the lives of others. These first three rules can be applied to anyone and can have an effect on a large number of individuals.

This rule, Collaborate to Be Great, moves you from working with larger groups to a smaller team and to guiding and directing individuals on that team to become good team players. This requires you to work closely and directly with team members. It asks you to personally become involved, to co-labor with others to achieve results. It mandates you to provide the right environment, the right direction, and the right degree of accountability to each so that the individual can grow and thus help the team grow. Succeed with this rule, and you'll be in leadership for a long time.

Let's define this rule a little further: collaboration is the action of working with others to produce or create. It's something that leaders who lead by position can't do, because collaboration does not occur in a command and control environment. Collaboration brings the leader and those they serve closer together, as the focus is not on the position but the task that needs to be completed. Collaboration allows a team to adapt to ever-changing conditions, it constantly keeps the big picture in view, and it cannot tolerate a win/lose mindset among the team.

Since collaboration involves more than one person, it affords more resources, ideas, and energy than would an individual. Collaboration brings complementary strengths to a leader, allowing a team to maximize a leader's potential and minimize his or her weaknesses. It can broaden and deepen a leader's ability to provide perspectives on how to meet or reach a goal, and collaboration can hold a leader more accountable.

> *Most great learning happens in groups. Collaboration is the stuff of growth.*
> –Ken Robinson

Collaboration occurs best on a team that has social harmony. The best place for collaboration is within a team that gets along, sees each other's viewpoints, communicates effectively, is committed to each other and the team, and can progress toward a common goal.

Your job is to grow such a team by developing the individuals on the team. Your ability to do this is what will separate your team as an effective team that gets results from those that are not effective and that struggle to see results. All things being equal, teams that can collaborate will significantly outperform teams that can't.

TEN PRINCIPLES OF TEAM COLLABORATION

But how can a leader get a team to collaborate? What must a leader do to really tap into the magnified power of team collaboration? How can one influence individuals to become strong team players?

While this is a skill that will take some time to develop, following the ten principles below will quicken your ability to achieve extraordinary results.

1. *If you build it, they will come.* *Building a vision gives confidence to the team.*

If you are old enough, you may recall the 1989 movie *Field of Dreams*. In this movie, Kevin Costner plays an Iowan farmer who hears a voice telling him to build a baseball stadium. The voice repeats the phrase "If you build it, they will come." Even though most people, including his wife, criticized him for such an idea, he built a stadium in the middle of a corn field. Just after completion, some of baseball's greats, appearing as ghosts, visited the new field, and hundreds of cars are traveling to the stadium as the movie closes. He built it, and they came.

Leadership is similar in that people want to follow a person with a vision. They want to be a part of something larger than themselves. They are looking for the person who can see the way. When a vision is clearly developed and articulated for an organization, people naturally start to align themselves toward that vision. Build it, and they will come.

Contrast this with a leader that has no vision. As I'm writing this, I'm staring at my fish tank. This tank is filled with about forty cichlids (a fish of African origin), moving in about forty different directions. They have no vision and are aimlessly moving from one end

> **Where there is no vision, the people perish.**
> –Proverbs 29:18

113

of the tank to the other. Leaders who have not built a vision have followers that are aimlessly moving around.

I have found that almost every employee is asking the following three questions:

- Where are we going?
- How are we going to get there?
- What is my role?

Creating a vision satisfies the first question, and it provides the basis for the next two questions. When people know where they are going, they become more confident about what they are doing. They also become more confident about the capabilities of the leader. Therefore, the first step in leading a collaborative team is building a vision.

2. **To win, you must pick winners.** *Choosing who will be on the team will greatly determine the success of the team.*

I'd like to say that I've always hired the best people, but unfortunately, that would not be true. In fact, I've made the mistake of hiring incorrectly numerous times. With only a three-month hiring season for teachers, I've hired too fast, not searched deep enough, thought that the mediocre candidate was the best I was going to find, or hired substandard teachers because I needed someone right then.

We all can come up with our own excuses why we've not done the work and taken the time we need to find the very best candidates, but the result is always the same. We complete the paperwork, conduct the onboarding, and pour a million resources into the new person, only to be unsatisfied with the results.

Now, we find a choice before us: do we accept the average, do we try to get rid of the person, or do we hire another to help do the job of the first? Choosing any of these three will result in a lose-lose situation. I've found that it is better to have an open spot on the team than to fill that spot with an ineffective team member.

To create a truly collaborative team, spend the time and take the efforts necessary to pick winners. Look for people that not only have the skills and knowledge necessary to do the job, but also have characteristics necessary to positively contribute to your team as a collaborative member.

Seek people who can communicate clearly and who are not afraid to express their ideas, but who do so in a caring and respectful way. Search out people who practice OB4S, who are willing to make personal sacrifices for the greater good, and who speak positively about others when they are not present.

I promise you, the more time and effort you spend up front in your selection of teammates, the more quickly you'll get to true collaboration—and the fewer headaches you'll have along the way.

3. *We all can't be the quarterback.* *All team members have a place where they are needed.*

George Reavis, previous superintendent of the Cincinnati Public Schools, used to tell this fable, written in 1940.

> Once upon a time, the animals decided they should do something meaningful to meet the problems of the new world. So, they organized a school. They adopted an activity curriculum of running, climbing, swimming, and flying. To make it fair and easier to administer, all the animals took all the subjects.
>
> The duck was excellent at swimming; in fact, he was better than his instructor was. However, he made only passing grades in flying and was very poor at running. Since he was so slow in running, he had to drop swimming and stay after school to practice running. This caused his webbed feet to be badly worn, so he became only average in swimming. But "average"

was acceptable; therefore, nobody worried about it—except the duck.

The rabbit started at the top of his class in running but developed a nervous twitch in his leg muscles, because he had so much makeup work to do in swimming.

The squirrel was excellent in climbing class, but he encountered constant frustration in flying class because his teacher made him start from the ground up instead of from the treetop down. He developed charley horses from overexertion, so he only got a "C" in climbing and a "D" in running.

The eagle was a problem child and was severely disciplined for being a non-conformist. In climbing classes, he beat all the others to the top, but insisted on using his own way of getting there!

The moral of this story is that everyone has strengths, but if we insist that people work in their areas of weakness, we will only get frustration and average results. Albert Einstein added, "Everyone is a genius. But if you judge a fish by its ability to climb a tree, it will live its whole life believing that it is stupid."

Imagine a football team. What if every player became the quarterback? That would be an absurd idea. A game of football occurs when you have a wide variety of talents and abilities couched perfectly into specific roles and responsibilities.

Influential leaders take the time to get to know the strengths of team members. They then find a spot where the individuals can use and develop their strengths. According to a recent Gallup poll, employees who use their strengths every day are six times more likely to be engaged in their work than their counterparts who are not in strength-using positions.[1] Six times!

Leaders who are serious about collaboration start by identifying the strengths of those on their teams. Marcus Buckingham, a world-recognized expert on strengths, says, "Most people think your strengths are what you're good at, and your weaknesses are what you're bad at." This is not the best way to identify strengths. What defines a strength, according to Buckingham, is an "activity [that] makes you feel strong;" it doesn't drain you but rather gives you energy.

There may be a lot of things that someone is good at but doesn't like doing. I'm reasonably good at analyzing data on an Excel spreadsheet; yet, after a few hours, I feel completely drained. Conversely, every time I get before an audience, I finish with more energy, more passion, and more drive than when I started. This is a strength.

To learn the strengths of those that you serve, spend time with them and discover the answers to these strength-finding questions.

1. What are they willing to stay after to get done?
2. What activities give them more energy?
3. What tasks would they volunteer to do without pay?
4. What are they aspiring to and why?
5. What sorts of hobbies do they have outside of work?
6. What clubs, groups, or organizations have they or do they belong to?

Identifying the strengths is only half the battle. Once you learn these, it behooves you to find a niche where they can use their strengths regularly. This is often difficult, as it may require a shift in employee positions, a change in the duties prescribed to titles, or the creation of new positions or duties that can capitalize on the individual's strengths.

> *Master your strengths. Outsource your weaknesses.*
> –Ryan Kahn

If they have no organizational skills, but are strong in creativity, don't put them in charge of planning events. Rather, find a place where they can have the freedom to run unrestricted with an idea. Do this, then step back and watch what happens.

Too often, leaders are not intentional about strengths and put people into positions that force them to draw upon their weaknesses. Why is this so? One common reason is time. Due to the busyness of the day, leaders don't take the time to learn about those on their team. Instead, they simply fill vacant positions or provide them with the same position descriptions that had been used for the last twenty years—both of which risk placing a person into a position of weakness.

Another mistake that leaders make is that they believe they can fix the weaknesses of those that they serve. They hope to at least make those they serve adequate at everything. Doing so will only make you and the individual frustrated, just as the duck was frustrated at having to quit swimming to run more.

As you increase the degree of your influence in helping individuals become strong team players, it is critical that you take the time and effort that is necessary to personally get to know those that you serve, determine their strengths, and find ways to magnify these in their duties, assignments, and roles.

4. Set the bar to go far. *Team members succeed when they clearly know what they are supposed to do.*

In the first principle of team collaboration, I mentioned that each employee is asking three questions: Where are we going? How are we going to get there? What is my role?

Setting the bar to go far answers this last question. If you want a high-performance team, then help each team member become crystal clear on duties and the expectations that you have.

Consultant and author Peter Drucker said, "One of the critical problems in the workplace today is that there is a lack of understanding between the employer and employee as to what the employee is to do. Often, employees are made to feel they are vaguely responsible for everything. It paralyzes them. Instead, we need to make clear to them what they are and are not responsible for. Then they will be able to focus their efforts on what we want, and they will succeed."

Furthermore, a 2016 Gallup poll found that just 29 percent of millennials are engaged in their jobs. The study suggests that they'd be much more committed if they received better job clarity and were held accountable for their performance.[2]

Influential leaders ensure that all members of the team understand their role. These leaders don't merely tell others what needs to be done, but they show how to get started and what the results will look like. Failing to do so is like asking a pole-vaulter to jump over the bar, without telling her how high it is set.

> *Clarity is crucial. Managers must keep expectations clear and to the point.*
> —Gallop

The clearer you can become in the general expectations of your team and the specific expectations of your individual team members, the more likely they are to meet these expectations.

At the junior high, when we were struggling with the behavior of students in the lunchroom and hallway, we'd often vent to each other that "these kids are so disrespectful" and that "students these days don't know how to act."

It was only after such griping that a teacher asked, "Well, have we explicitly told them what we expect, and have we showed them what that would look like?"

We all looked at each other and shrugged our shoulders. We then developed a plan to identify specific actions that equate appropriate behavior in the hallways and lunchroom and then taught the students by showing them what the behavior looked like. The results were astounding. They became considerably more respectful and appropriate.

Be sure that job descriptions, expectations, and roles are completely understood for each of those that you serve. Provide them written explanations, but also coach them through their duties by telling them and showing them what you mean.

5. **The goal is more important than the role.** *Team members understand that the objective is more important than their title or position.*

Living in Minnesota, there are a few weeks each fall when all day long you can hear a certain sound: the honking of overhead geese. Literally, hundreds of these geese fly over my house every year as they start their thousand-mile migration to the warmth of the southern states.

One day, as I was watching several groups fly over, I got curious and decided to do some research. I observed that all geese migrate in a "V" formation and learned that research has revealed some fascinating facts as to why:

- When each bird flaps its wings, it creates an uplift for the bird immediately behind it.
- When the lead goose, who is exerting more effort than the rest, gets tired, he rotates to the back and allows another goose to fly in the lead position.
- During flight, each of the geese honk from behind to encourage those up front to keep up their speed.

By traveling in a "V" formation, the whole flock can add up to a 71 percent increase in flying range, compared to an individual bird flying alone. Whoever said "Silly goose" was seriously mistaken. There is nothing silly about this. Geese have mastered the ability to collaborate and reap the benefits of this collaboration every fall and every spring.

An important principle that we can learn from geese is that their desire to reach their destination supersedes any role. To put this into business terms, when we are firmly focused upon a goal, our roles tend to take a secondary position.

Not long ago, I was working with a group that provided staffing for the 2018 Super Bowl. To successfully meet the expectations, many of the staff members took on tasks that were not part of their traditional job descriptions. Some managers stepped into entry-level roles, some in marketing helped with filling positions, and others in sales ended up supervising on-site teams. To this team, the goal of ensuring a full staff for the Super Bowl was much more important than their titled responsibilities.

As I think about this principle, I'm reminded of a picture I saw where the white line indicating the side of a road was painted around a tree that had partially fallen into the road. I can imagine what the painter of road lines probably thought as he approached this fallen tree: "My job is to paint lines. Moving trees, not my job. I'll just go around it." Seeing a problem but not owning it is a violation of this principle. This is not what geese do, it's not what the staffing agency did, and it absolutely must not be what your team does. Working on a team means stepping into different roles to meet the goal.

As an influential leader who is building collaboration, it is your job to help others individually understand the vision. It's your job to establish the expectations that you have of them for meeting that vision. And, it's your job to ensure that the responsibility of meeting and achieving of the vision is felt by everyone, leaders and team members. We all need to have flexibility and a willingness to do whatever is necessary to achieve the vision.

6. **Always be ready to answer the question "Are we there yet?"** *Knowing where you are allows people to make adjustments and move forward.*

Fifteen times over the past two decades, my wife and I, with our four kids in tow, have driven the 2,400 miles cross country to visit my parents and extended family in Utah. We've learned something from all those miles: knowing exactly where we were at any given moment is valuable information. Knowing where we were gave us the ability to determine how much patience we needed, to know when to stop, where to eat, what rest areas were ahead, how long it was going to be until the next gas station, what roads to take, and it gave us the answer the never-ending question: "Are we there yet?"

Knowing where we were also provided to Sarah and me the ability to quickly assess the situation and adjust if necessary. We could stop earlier for food, fill up the tank, get out and stretch, put in a movie, play a game, or inspect the car for safety. It also helped the kids understand the adjustments they needed to make.

I fear that, too often, leaders "hop in the car" and start their cross-country journey without taking the time that is necessary to watch the mile markers. They get excited about refining a process, starting a new initiative, bringing in a new software system, or making any other changes without stopping and pinpointing exactly where the organization, and each person, is in relation to the overall vision. It's like a basketball coach that can't see the scoreboard, nor can he explain how each team member has contributed to the score.

Identifying individual contributions and using mile markers does not have to be rocket science. In fact, it is easy once you know what you are looking for. Let's go back again to the three questions every employee is asking.

1) **Where are we going?**

This is expressed through your vision. As a leader, you are constantly creating a picture of the vision for those you serve, through conversations, visuals, newsletters, team meetings, emails, presentations, and every other form of communication available.

2) **How are we going to get there?**

Determining who will be on your team (principle two) and what strengths everyone has (principle three) will help with this question.

3) **What's my role?**

Establishing clear expectations for individual team members (principle four) and helping them understand that meeting the goal supersedes the role (principle five) provides the understanding that is necessary for them to adequately answer this third question.

I'd now like to add one more question onto these three. This may not be a question that you would naturally ask, but it is certainly one that everyone thinks about.

4) **How am I doing?**

Being able to answer this question gives the leader a powerful edge and taking the time to answer each of the previous three questions provides to the leader the ability to do so. If you've developed the big picture, identified how you are to achieve the big picture, and concretely detailed each person's role in moving toward the big picture, then all that is left is to become observant, take notes, and document how everyone is doing.

This really is a matter of paying attention, of looking outside the window to see the green mile markers, and then keeping a record of what you've seen. A common mistake of beginner leaders is to delay this fourth question until just before a performance evaluation is due. Typically, this means that you only pay specific attention to the individuals' contributions (or lack thereof) once per year. That's like driving a thousand miles without looking to see where you are.

Ponder this: a jet flying toward a destination is off course 99 percent of the time due to wind, altitude, turbulence, and weather. Pilots and automated equipment use hundreds of indicators to constantly course-correct. Ignoring only one degree off course will result in a flight from New York to Los Angeles to land at John Wayne Airport, fifty miles south. Don't be the leader that lands in the wrong airport. Be sure to know where each individual is and frequently share this information so that everyone can make the appropriate course corrections.

*7. **Care to Confront.** Giving feedback to team members strengthens the chain.*

I've asked a lot of leaders what the hardest part of their jobs is. Almost without exception, having critical feedback conversations ranks in the top three of the most difficult things leaders have to do.

I typically follow up by asking, "Why is this so difficult?" Most responses to this question will fall into one of three areas: selfishness, worry, or ignorance.

Selfishness. Often leaders do not provide critical feedback because they believe that it will change the way that the employee sees the leader. Leaders like to be liked, and the assumption that some leaders make is that if they deliver negative feedback, the employee will no longer like the leader. While this may be true in some situations, if you are honest and helpful in your critical feedback, the individual will like you even more, as you're striving to help them become a better person.

Worry About Response. Sometimes, leaders do not provide critical feedback because they are worried about the response of the individual. Will they start crying? Will they get upset and start yelling? Will they retaliate in some way? Will this break their self-esteem?

> *Care about people's approval, and you will always be their prisoner.*
> —Lao Tzu

The answer to these questions is yes, they will. It's only natural to have an emotional response when we get feedback about ourselves. Sometimes, people will cry, yell, or retaliate, yet this should not stop us from providing the feedback.

Recall the hammer principle when I mentioned that we sometimes have to tear down to build up? I referenced that in building muscle, you must repeatedly lift heavy enough weight to tear the muscle down. Then, during your rest period, and with the proper nutrition, the muscle grows back stronger.

You don't stop lifting because your muscles are screaming; you push through the pain, knowing that growth is on the other side. The same goes for people. When we care enough to confront and have difficult conversations, we acknowledge that it may cause some pain but understand that great growth can be gained from the pain.

Lack of knowledge. Many beginner leaders do not confront because they don't know how. They don't know what to say, how to say it, or how to provide support while giving criticism. They have not taken the time nor experienced the training that can give them the know-how and the confidence to have these conversations. Therefore, they often ignore the issue or assume that it will resolve itself with time.

If you find yourself wondering if you know what to do, allow me to share with you six steps to giving feedback that will not only provide knowledge but also give you the confidence to get started.

1. Confront ASAP.

The longer you wait, the less likely it is that you will confront. Even if it might be something small, acting promptly will save those you lead from being blindsided when you may have to do something formally.

In the beginning of my leadership, I was scared to confront, because I worried about the other person's response. Therefore, I'd see something that someone would do—something small—and either pretend that I didn't see it or simply ignore it. Then they would do it again, and again, and again. Eventually, this "small thing" turned into a big thing, which led to a conversation that was much more difficult than it needed to be. Remember the plane analogy? It's much easier to make a one-degree course correction than a twenty-degree correction.

2. Acknowledge strengths.

Begin the conversation by letting them know how valuable they are to the team. Express your appreciation for the work that they do.

Let them know of the strengths that you see in them. Do all of this with the upmost sincerity. Dale Carnegie, in the book *How to Win Friends and Influence People,* said that "Beginning with praise is like a dentist that begins his work with Novocain. The patient still gets a drilling, but the Novocain is pain-killing."

Then, without using the words "but" or "however," move onto the next step. For example: "Dan, thanks for meeting with me today. I am so grateful that you are on our team, and I really appreciate all the time that you put into that report last week. (Avoid saying but or however here). The reason that we are meeting today is that I have some questions…"

3. Ask questions.

Before you make any concluding judgements about their behavior, keep an open mind and ask a few questions to see if there is information you are missing. "The reason we are meeting today is that I have copies of some emails that seem to carry a pretty negative tone regarding the implementation of our new initiative. Would you mind telling me your thoughts about this change?" Take the time that is necessary and continue to ask questions before you move to the next step. Your goal is to help them self-identify both the problem and how to improve.

4. Clearly articulate the issue.

If they can identify the issue through your questioning, confirm their conclusion. Restate your expectations and the specifics as to how they did not meet your expectations. If they did not come to this understanding on their own, inform them of the issue with evidence (show them the emails, point out language that makes you interpret their message as negative).

During this stage, be very careful to avoid words like "always" and "never." Even if they seem to "always" be late, there is probably an instance or two when they were on time. Furthermore, these two words are sure to put the other person on the defensive, which isn't conducive for a constructive conversation.

5. Provide direction.

If your questioning has helped them see how they could improve, restate what they have said and express that this is how you'd suggest they get better, too. If not, explicitly describe the steps that they would need to take to get better. Give examples and be specific in your explanation. "If you would use a sentence like this one or if you'd replace that word with this one, it would sound a lot more positive." Ask them to commit to making the change by following the steps discussed.

6. Show care and confidence.

Finally, don't end the meeting without expressing to them your care for them as a person and the confidence you have in them making a change. If you cannot express genuine confidence, I suggest you go back to chapter three. "Again, Dan, thanks for meeting with me. I really am appreciative to have you on the team, and I know that you can take these steps to more positively support our team's initiative."

You've probably heard the adage "A chain is only as strong as its weakest link." This is frequently used in relation to teams, meaning that a team is only as strong as its weakest member. While I don't like the idea of identifying the "weakest link," I do think that it is the responsibility of a leader to help each of their team members to grow, especially if they are heading off course or are not in alignment with the team's vision.

Collaboration depends upon all team members working cohesively, being committed to the objective, and giving their very best to the project. Influential leaders meet individually with each of their team

> We all need people who will give us feedback. That's how we improve.
> —Bill Gates

127

members, providing to them feedback that can help them grow. They constantly are answering question number four, "How am I doing?".

Don't take this principle too lightly. To create individuals that are great team players, you must have the care that is necessary to confront. You must recognize that people will not just get better on their own. You must accept that it is your duty to begin and engage people in these kinds of discussions. Some of my most valued relationships are with people whom I've had such conversations. True, this is one of the hardest things about leadership, yet there is little else that has the possibility for positive impact.

8. Groupthink can really stink. *Trust and transparency allow all voices to be heard.*

I recall an initiative that I was trying to get started at a school a few years ago. We were struggling with helping students who were failing multiple courses, and I'd devised a method that would provide frequent updates on the learning objectives for each of these students, along with an after-school support program to help them achieve the learning objectives.

I brought this idea to the school's leadership team. I took time to explain why we needed it and how it solved each of our needs. I then asked if people had questions. Since there were none, I moved that we start this program. Everyone nodded their heads in the affirmative, and we ended the meeting with me feeling wonderful about how we are going to help students.

Over the next few weeks, I noticed, sadly, that, even though they agreed to the change in our meeting, their actions stated otherwise. No one did a thing! There was no action, no follow-through on the intervention steps, and no help for the struggling kids. For the most part, the only thing that did happen was negative backchannel conversations about my idea. What went wrong?

One explanation is that our team got trapped into the tragedy of groupthink, an idea developed by Irving Janis, a research psychologist from Yale University. He used this idea to help explain why people in group meetings go along with decisions that they object to or think are bad. He quoted one classic experience from American history: The Bay of Pigs.

Janis argued that when the Kennedy administration took over, it "uncritically accepted" a proposed idea from a high-ranking general to arm the Cubans with guns so that they could overthrow their dictator, Fidel Castro. When the decision was made, many in the room disagreed with it or thought it was going to be a mistake ... but they said nothing. They dared not oppose the president or the high-ranking general, so they went along with it. Unfortunately, there were no Cubans waiting around for the U.S. to covertly begin a coup against their dictator. In the end, this was one of America's greatest moments of embarrassment.[3]

> **When we all think alike, no one thinks very much.**
> –Albert Einstein

Unfortunately, the entire decision-making group fell victim of groupthink. Even more unfortunate is that if they understood what groupthink was, the entire embarrassment could have been avoided.

Groupthink can be defined as a psychological phenomenon within a group where the desire for harmony or conformity results in an inexpression of ideas or a public agreement, while retaining a private opposition.

Take my leadership team as an example. There were many at the table who disagreed with the idea, some who had ways to improve the idea, and others who outright opposed the idea based upon their contract. Yet, they all nodded in non-verbal agreement to the idea. That is, they all conformed for fear of expressing opposition. The reason for this—a lack of trust!

To get all members of a team to collaborate, you need to hear all the voices of the team, even the opposing ones. Patrick Lencioni, author of *The Five Dysfunctions of a Team*, asserts that the two greatest dysfunctions of teams are a lack of trust and the fear of conflict. Put both of these together and you'll get groupthink.

The more that leaders can develop trust on a team and the more that they can hear all voices, even those that may be opposed from the majority, the better the leaders will be able to avoid groupthink.

As I reflected on my experience with the new initiative and the school's leadership team, a lack of trust was certainly an issue. This led me to becoming frustrated in our failed attempt at my new initiative.

If everyone agrees, ask yourself two questions 1) Have I created a culture where it is safe for people to express opposing viewpoints? and 2) Have I been able to hear everyone's honest voice?

If members of your team do not share their opinions frequently and openly, there may be a lack of trust. Influential leaders will carefully observe who is talking and who is not talking. They will have conversations with individuals outside of the meeting about their feelings regarding trust on the team. These leaders will encourage the team members to openly share their ideas during team meetings.

For some teams, it can be a great challenge to get someone to speak up. Since everyone's input is extremely valuable, in these cases, influential leaders devise methods to ensure that all voices are heard. For example, instead of asking for verbal agreement or openly voting on an idea, have people write down their vote. Another strategy is to have team members brainstorm on an idea before the meeting. They then either send to you their ideas, or they bring in their brainstorming sheet to share with others.

The power of allowing people to have a voice is incredible. First, they feel like they matter, because you've asked for their input. Second, they feel like they have contributed to the team. Third, even though the final decision of the team may not be in support of what was inputted, they often are more committed, because their voice has been heard. While it may take a little extra time, seeking to hear all voices will certainly help you avoid the stink of groupthink.

9. You can't go along unless you all get along. *Effective teams take responsibility for unity.*

Probably one of the most annoying things I experience as a leader is when someone comes to me with thoughts about another person, otherwise known as gossip. Typically, these thoughts are not illegal in nature, but rather relate to more minor things or to feelings: "I just don't like it when she assumes that…," "He is not pulling his weight on this project," or "You should let her know that she offended me."

True collaborative teams are teams that own the responsibility for cohesiveness. They don't constantly run to the leader to solve every interpersonal problem. Rather, they place the responsibility of working together on their own shoulders. These teams have the trust and the confidence to call each other out, to address offenses and hurt feelings, and to speak openly with each other.

> *Team unity and team chemistry are by far more important than talent.*
> —Rob Colbert

This is not something that can happen overnight. No team ever wakes up a day or two after being formed and finds that everyone has accepted the responsibility for unity. In fact, for most teams, there will be times of frustration and anger before this responsibility is ever accepted.

As an influential leader, strive to help individuals own the responsibility of team unity. Care to confront individuals who cause team disruption, even if they are great producers.

If you find yourself being the go-between for interpersonal team issues, try the 24-hour rule.

When a person approaches you with a problem, a concern, some gossip, or an ill feeling about another person, inform them that they have 24 hours to address the problem themselves or you will do it for them.

It goes like this, "Sally, I'm sorry that she offended you. Now, you've got 24 hours from this moment to talk to her about it, or I'll have a meeting with her and let her know what you've expressed to me."

This rule does two things. First, it will greatly reduce the comments coming your way, because most will not consider it important enough to be addressed so formally. They may be offended but just wanted to complain to you, not to have the issue revealed. This reduces some of the minutia of leadership and opens the door for issues of a more serious nature.

Second, this encourages your team members to solve their own problems, to talk about their feelings and attitudes with each other, and to come to resolutions without your intervention.

Once you've modeled this for others, ask your team to do it with each other. Suddenly, you'll notice that almost all behind-the-back complaining about others will disappear. Once this is removed, your team's likelihood of collaborating is greatly enhanced.

10. *Momentum is a team's best friend.* *Teams find a way to win and to keep winning.*

For sports enthusiasts, one of the most exciting times of the year is March Madness. This is when sixty-eight Division One college basketball teams enter a single elimination bracket to determine who the top team of the year is.

The reason this is one of the most exciting times is that almost anything can happen. It is not uncommon for a low-seeded team to get an early win and catch fire, proceeding to the final four or even the championship—beating out those that are ranked a lot higher to do so. This happens frequently enough that there is a name for it: the

Cinderella team. How can teams accomplish this? Simple, they develop momentum.

Momentum is a forward movement that requires a great force to stop. Momentum is energy. It's power, and once created, it becomes one of the greatest forces a team can harness.

Consider this: a team without momentum sees any problem as an insurmountable challenge. They get deflated, are not motivated, and avoid trying to solve the problem at all costs. This happens with big problems, little problems, and even problems that aren't really problems. A team without momentum is like a train stopped on the tracks, with a lot of potential power but no forward movement. When the locomotive does start to move, even the smallest block of steel could stop it again.

A team with momentum is quite the opposite. They don't see problems; they see challenges. They get energized, excited, and passionate about what might appear to be insurmountable. A team with momentum is like a locomotive traveling at sixty miles per hour. Even a five-foot-thick block of reinforced cement could not stop them.

So how do you get momentum? What does a leader have to do to get the wheels of the train moving? Much of what is discussed in this chapter is intentionally designed to generate momentum. You start with a big vision, surround yourself with winners, find and utilize the strengths of your team, establish expectations and evaluation criteria, and hold people accountable. All these actions will get you moving, but let's not stop there. Allow me to suggest two additional ideas.

If you are like most people, you want immediate results. For example, you join the gym, dutifully work out five times a week for two weeks and hope to be fit or you put some money in the stock market and want to see it grow rapidly.

This desire makes sense, as our society has taught us that we can get things immediately: instant coffee, instant oatmeal, fast food, almost any movie on demand, and packages delivered to our house in just one day.

> Keep moving ahead because action creates momentum, which in turn creates unanticipated opportunities.
> –Nick Vujicic

Unfortunately, this is not how life works, and it is definitely not how you build momentum. Momentum isn't created in an instant. Momentum takes intentional effort and it takes time. They say a champion is only recognized in the ring, meaning that the momentum was started much earlier in the daily practices over the course of years. Thus, the key to creating momentum is consistency. It's working at it day after day, month after month, year after year and not giving up.

If you've ever watched a train start from a dead stop, you've noticed that it begins to move very slowly and gradually, over time, it increases in speed. When it comes to building your team, you can't expect instant success. This is a process of working with individuals on specific things, over a course of time to build up speed and momentum. In the next chapter, I'll take some time to elaborate how we can work with individuals to build momentum on a team.

When teams and individuals do start to move, it's critical for building momentum to encourage the movement through celebration.

Celebration is when influential leaders pay very close attention to the initial collaborative steps toward a team's objective. The leader then ensures that they recognize and reward these initial small victories. If you think you should wait until the train is speeding at sixty miles per hour to recognize and reward, you'll be waiting a very long time, because it will probably never happen.

Start to celebrate as soon as you hit one mile per hour. When you've made a decision, celebrate. When you've accomplished your first objective (no matter how small), celebrate. When people find their strengths, celebrate. When someone puts the goal above his or her role, celebrate.

Make no mistake; taking the time early on to recognize and celebrate the achievements of the team will provide the steam that starts momentum. Mary Kay Ash, the genius behind the Mary Kay cosmetic company, said that "there are only two things that people want more than money and sex: praise and recognition."

Influential leaders will ensure that all efforts toward building a strong team and moving toward its objectives are recognized. They will also intentionally set, look for, and reward results. Have fun with this, make it into a contest, celebrate in unique or even ridiculous ways, and make it public. You'll soon be leading a train that can't be stopped.

As we conclude this chapter, let me reemphasize that when you're all pulling together, you'll get outstanding results. This only occurs when you, as a leader, help individuals to become team players. Dale Carnegie said, "It marks a big step in our development when you come to realize that other people can help you do a better job than you could do alone." Make a resolution now that you will help everyone on your team to become collaborative team players so that you can get outstanding results.

YOKING YOUR TEAM

☐ **Describe your vision.** In three sentences or less, describe your vision. What objective are you collaborating toward?

_____

_____

_____

_____

☐ **Create an S/D chart.** Take out a sheet of paper and fold it into thirds. Unfold it, and on the far-left third, write down the names of everyone on your team. In the middle section, list the STRENGTHS of each team member. On the far right, list what job DUTIES they have that use their strengths. You may notice some gaps. Take the next two weeks to fill in these gaps. Find a template for this at www.i2eyesquared.com/resources.

☐ **Validate the voices.** In your next team meeting, instead of publicly voting on a decision or simply asking if there are any questions about a decision, hand each person a slip of paper. Ask them to cast their vote or create a question about a potential decision. Gather the papers and have a group discussion.

☐ **Celebrate a win.** Take a moment right now—get a card and write a note to someone, expressing your appreciation for a contribution to your team. If you don't have a card, order some and make this a weekly practice.

Name of Person: _____

Reason for Note: _____

_____

_____

Rule Number Five

INCREASE CAPACITY TO INCREASE INFLUENCE

May you stay in one place forever.

—An ancient Tartar curse

T wo days after my sixteenth birthday, I started my first job. I was a bag boy at a local grocery store. On my first day, I met Larry, my new manager. Larry was a tall, skinny, and socially-awkward middle-aged man. He struggled at making connections, but somehow, he and I bonded. Over the two years of my employment at this grocery store, he taught me much of what I know about success.

One of his best lessons was about staying busy. He taught that when you are on the clock, you should always be doing something productive. Even now, I can still hear him saying, "If you've got time to lean, you've got time to clean." This was an important lesson for a young bagger boy. There was a lot of downtime in the role, and most of the other bag boys would just waste time, putting fruitless hours on the clock. But he taught me to behave differently. He taught me to re-shelve items, take out the garbage, restock the receipt paper, straighten the shelves, and sweep the floors.

My favorite was when he showed me a long PVC pipe that had a ball of tape at the top of it. He grabbed the pipe from its leaning position against the wall, handed it to me, and said, "Jason, we've got a balloon problem. They have escaped from their balloon cage and are all around the store. Go and use this pole to catch them and then return them to their home."

For Larry, there never was time to stop doing. Life was not about wasting away down time, but rather using the time to better the store, to better the experience of others, and to better ourselves. He never believed in being comfortable, settling for the status quo, or becoming content with who we are. His was always an uphill battle, a mission to improve himself, and everything around him.

> *Growth and self-transformation cannot be delegated.*
> –Lewis Mumford

Some leaders are quite the opposite to Larry. They fall into the temptation to slow down once they've received their title. They believe that because they have worked hard to get into a certain position, they don't have to continue to work hard; they can now simply enjoy the benefits of their efforts. They become okay with the way things are. They've reached the "destination," and now they are going on "vacation."

Leaders of influence recognize that to keep influence, they must constantly be growing and helping others to grow. They cannot be satisfied with status quo. They refuse to take the vacation. After reaching the top, they find a higher mountain and start to ascend again. They look for things they can do to make things better, to return the balloons back to their home.

You see, you cannot give what you don't have, you can't teach what you don't know, and you can't lead others to places you've never been. To lead, you must continuously improve. To increase in influence, you must increase your capacity. If Larry were still around today, he might say it this way: "If you have time to burn, you have time to learn," and learning will increase your capacity, and thus, you can increase the capacity of others.

By following these last two rules of influential leadership, we can move ourselves and others to new levels of living, to a higher state of understanding, and to a greater degree of performance. We will become leaders who have positively impacted the lives of those we lead through our influence, and they will thank us for what we have helped them become. Therefore, we increase in influence through our efforts to help others increase in their capacity.

THE TOUR GUIDE PRINCIPLE

Have you ever considered the differences between a tour guide and a travel agent?

Several years ago, Sarah and I decided to go on a cruise. We were to spend seven days in the sun in the Caribbean. Our port of call was Puerto Rico, and when our plane landed, we had nearly six hours before we had to be on the ship. With this extra time, we headed out to the streets and found Jorge, a small tour bus driver. The eight of us nearly filled his bus, and over the next three hours, Jorge gave us the time of our life! He took us to the best shopping areas, the historical sites, and the famous landmarks.

But he did much more than that, too. He also showed us the hidden secrets of the island, the places of local historical significance, the authentic shops, and explained to us the "behind the scenes" of the tourist industry. It was fascinating.

In fact, we were enjoying our time with Jorge so much that we nearly skipped our cruise so that we could spend more time with him. Why? Why was this three-hour experience so grand? It was amazing because, although Jorge had grown up on the island, he never became satisfied with all he knew or had experienced. He avidly sought additional information, and he persistently learned as much as he could about the island so that he could teach others. As a result, he was one of the most sought-after tour guides in Puerto Rico.

> *In this world, you're either growing or you're dying, so get in motion and grow.*
> –Lou Holtz

After returning from our cruise, I recognized that this experience could have been very different. We could have contacted a travel agency, we could have asked them what there was to do on the island, and they could have given us a bunch of brochures and told us what to do.

Most likely, compared to our experience with Jorge, using a travel agency would not have been nearly as fascinating. It was Jorge, the tour guide, that made this an unforgettable trip.

What then is the difference between what could have been and what occurred—between enlisting a travel agency or hiring a tour guide? It's simple, really. A travel agent shows you several wonderful places (many of which he or she may have never been to), points, and says, "Go there." A tour guide pulls the bus off to the side of the road, opens the door, and says, "Let's go."

When we take the time to develop our capacity as leaders, we are moving away from being a travel agent and becoming more and more like Jorge, an experienced and educated tour guide who opens the door for others. Leadership expert John Maxwell states, "Leaders know the way, go the way, and show the way."

Tour guides know the way because they have personally gone down the pathway; they have had the experiences. Because of this, they can effectively show people the pathway. Think about your current leadership style. Using the chart below, are you more like a travel agent or a tour guide?

Travel Agent Leadership	Tour Guide Leadership
Tells people what to do	Shows people what to do
Gives advice	Gives experiences
Remains in a comfortable office	Gets out to the "field"
Asks people to do what they've not done themselves	Goes first and asks others to follow
Gives people fish	Teaches others to fish
Offers knowledge	Offers wisdom
Points and says, "Go"	Opens the door and says, "Let's go"

The Tour Guide Principle says that *leaders open the door and take others with them.* Deciding now to be a tour guide, to increase your capacity, places you into a position where you can have a profound positive impact on those that you lead by bringing them along with you on the leadership-development road.

GROWTH DOESN'T JUST HAPPEN

Here's a hard truth: some people question the need for a tour guide. They look at life and simply assume that they will grow. They assume that others will grow, too. They think that growth just naturally happens. They observe a child and recognize that, with almost no effort, beyond daily food and water, the child goes from a small infant to a small human being who is able to walk and talk. They think that our learning, that the development of our brains and our capacity, happens in the same way.

What most adults have forgotten is how hard they worked at school to grow in intelligence and experience. If you have school-age kids currently, you know what I mean. If you don't, go back in time with me for a minute.

Many kids wake up around 6:30 a.m. to get ready for the school day. They head off to school around 7:30, with most schools starting around 8:00. Then, for the next six-and-a-half hours, they attend classes, where they strive to grow and learn. Sure, there are a few breaks for recess, lunch, and gym, but even if you take these out, you are still actively learning for nearly five hours a day. Around 3:00 p.m., they get on the bus to come home. Typically, they will take a break at home and then get right back to learning, whether that be through doing their homework, practicing a musical instrument, or reading a book.

In short, the typical kid is spending somewhere between five to eight hours a day actively learning. Eventually, they end up graduating, and many decide to enroll in college, where the number of active learning hours increases significantly. Growth was very intentional during our formal education days; it didn't just happen on its own.

Unfortunately, many people graduate from high school or finish college and decide that they're done with learning. They've figured that the efforts put in during their school days are all that they need for success, and now, they should focus on doing their jobs, and they will turn out just fine. This is a terribly wrong assumption for at least three reasons.

First, our mind is like a muscle: if we use it, it strengthens; if we don't use it, it gets weak. This was clearly evident when I'd welcome students back into my classroom after a summer break. It took weeks and sometimes months for me to get their brains back into shape. I would even notice differences after the winter and spring breaks. It's like dystrophy of the mind set in any time they were not exercising their minds. Due to the rigor of formal education, we often finish with a strong mind, yet if we don't intentionally continue that learning, we will lose what we once had.

Second, we live in a modern society where new knowledge is produced at an ever-increasingly rapid rate. Perhaps a hundred years ago, you could get away with relying solely upon the knowledge you gained through formal primary education. However, in today's society, that knowledge quickly becomes outdated, leaving you and your abilities behind in the dust.

> *Change is inevitable, but personal growth is a choice.*
> –Bob Proctor

From a leadership perspective, this is really about credibility. For about the first six months on the other side, your ability to connect will override the need for credibility. Then during the next six months, this will shift, and your credibility will override your ability to connect. To be credible, you must constantly be learning by being intentional in your personal development.

Third, we will suffer from a lack of motivation. This may seem a little counterintuitive, as it takes motivation to learn. How can learning create motivation? Isn't it supposed to be the other way around? Not so. Learning new things provides to our brains novelty, and our brains react positively to this by releasing dopamine.

You've probably heard of this chemical before. It is often touted as the reward chemical, and it rewards indeed. However, more recent research has shown that dopamine is more closely related to the seeking of rewards rather than receiving the reward itself.

What that means is that when we learn, we get dopamine, which causes us to have the desire, or the motivation, to learn more. This learning then increases our understanding, which increases our capacity, which then increases our ability to attain success, in leadership or in any other area of life. If you question this, pay close attention to your motivation levels following an episode of your favorite TV sitcom, compared to watching an engaging documentary about the planet earth. When we become intentional in our learning, we will quickly see that learning provides to us motivation.

In short, growth just does not happen—you must be intentional.

DEVELOPING AN INTENTIONAL GROWTH PLAN

The importance of intentionally increasing my capacity hit me three years after completing my undergraduate degree. At that time, I started to feel something missing, I felt a lack of motivation, and I didn't have clear direction. I went to college, got my degree, and started teaching, but I noticed myself getting comfortable after a few years. Yes, teaching students is very challenging, but the curriculum is repetitive, and once you've taught the same thing five times a day, three years in a row, you start to relax a little, to stop putting in as much effort as before.

One day, when I was talking to the students about the importance of being a lifelong learner, I was struck with this thought: "Jason, you've stopped learning ... you're not being a lifelong learner, so how can you preach this to others?"

The internal realization of hypocrisy broke me from my temporary complacency. I jumped back into reading a few broccoli books (books that are good for the mind), and I started to formulate what I eventually called an Intentional Growth Plan, or IGP.

Creating an IGP really is not complicated, it's only a description of an area that you'd like to grow in and how you are going to grow in it. Sounds easy, right? Yet less than 3 percent of Americans have even committed the first step (what they want) to paper. Not surprisingly, this 3 percent also includes the most successful, most wealthy, and most satisfied people in our society.

How can we really grow unless we have a plan? Can you imagine a basketball team heading out to the court to compete against their rivals, only to find that there are no basketball hoops? It would not make sense, and neither would it make sense to be a leader without an Intentional Growth Plan.

As we walk out onto the basketball court of life, it is our responsibility to ensure that there is a plan, that we know our areas of capacity, what we are going to do to grow our capacity, and how we can measure it.

Remember, growth just doesn't happen; you must be intentional, and developing an IGP is an outward expression of your inward intentionality for improvement.

My first Intentional Growth Plan had seven categories of life: mental, physical, career, family, financial, spiritual, and personal.

I then identified a learning goal for each area, along with stepping stones that I could take, obstacles that might get in my way, and what I was going to do to resolve and overcome those obstacles. The results can speak for themselves.

I set a goal to become a principal eight years from the time I made my growth plan. I achieved it in five. I set an income goal over the six-figure mark, and I met it in six years instead of the planned nine. I finished a master's degree six months earlier than I had planned and became a public speaker earlier, too. I don't say this to impress you, but rather to impress upon you the power of having a written IGP.

If you've not developed a growth plan, read through the following five steps and then stop reading this book. This rule of leadership is so valuable that I'm asking you to make it a top priority.

Besides, this chapter is going to ask you to lead others by helping them develop a plan, and any leader should be willing to go down a pathway before they ask another to do the same.

Take a lesson from Gandhi. One Sunday, a woman came up to Gandhi and asked him if he could speak to her son and convince him to stop eating too many sweets.

Gandhi replied that he could not but asked the woman to come back one week later and make the same request.

The next Sunday, the woman approached Gandhi and repeated her initial request, to which he responded, "I can now do this."

Confused, she asked, "Why can you do this now when you couldn't do it a week ago?"

He replied, "Because one week ago, I too was eating too many sweets."

Creating an intentional plan will give you the credibility to ask others to do the same.

Let's take a closer look at how we can create an Intentional Growth Plan by using the **DAILY** strategy. **DAILY** represents five steps that every good growth plan contains.

> **D** – Determine What You Want to Learn
> **A** – Assess Your Capacity
> **I** – Identify Action Steps
> **L** – Live the Actions Daily
> **Y** – Yourself Hold Accountable

Determine What You Want to Learn.

Most of us have already put some thought into what we really want. Most fathers want to be a good father, most managers want to be a good leader, and most entry-level employees want to climb the ladder, but you need to determine what you should learn to achieve what you want.

For example, to be a good father, you may consider learning about discipline techniques. To be a good leader, you may want to improve your ability to communicate, and to climb the ladder, you may want to learn time management skills.

Assess Your Capacity.

Determine how good you are in this area of your life. How good are you at discipline? How would you rate your ability to communicate? On a scale of one to ten, where would you put your ability to manage your time?

You may want to consider getting other people involved for this step. Find a trusted person who is strong in the area you want to grow in and ask for their feedback about how you can improve.

When I first started my speaking and training business, I knew that I would need to be strong in sales. Although I have never formally been in sales, I had "sold" social studies to teenagers for many years, and I thought that it wouldn't be too hard to pick up the skills. Nevertheless, I knew that I was going to need some help, so I searched our community for someone who was a master at sales.

After some effort, I found a vice president of sales for a regional staffing agency and asked him to be my mentor. I had to offer to train his leadership staff at no cost, but he agreed and helped me assess my ability to sell.

Identify Action Steps.

If you'd like to be a better leader, simply deciding to improve your communication skills is not enough. The guts of a person's IGP are the action steps that they will take to increase in capacity. For example, you may decide to read a book on body language, to start listening to podcasts on charisma, or to attend a seminar on making communication simpler and more effective.

This step asks you to identify specifically what you are going to do to grow. This is the main body of your growth plan. Ideas could include reading books, listening to podcasts, and attending events, like mentioned above. It could also include learning about a topic online, watching YouTube videos, starting a book study, forming an online discussion group, listening to audio recordings, or finding a mentor. There are an infinite number of activities that you can do for self-improvement.

Try to identify three to four specific learning activities that are directly tied to what you want to learn. The more specific you can be with the action steps, the more quickly you'll see an increase in your capacity.

<u>L</u>ive the Actions Daily.

This is the most important step of them all—and the area of greatest violation for most people. Often, we determine our action steps and say things like "I'll get started sometime;" "Once a week, I will;" or "I'm going to do this twice a month." These are all good statements, because they show positive intention, but I believe that if we don't make our growth a <u>daily</u> priority, we will find other priorities that will push our intentions aside.

The best IGP's have a determination of what we can do on a daily basis. For example, I read, write, file, and reflect daily. Every day, I spend at least 30 minutes in a book that relates to my area of learning. Every day, I write on topics that I train on. Every day, I file quotes, ideas, and resources into Evernote. Every day, I reflect in a journal.

Failure to take action daily will result in a loss of your ability to learn. Conversely, being consistent each and every day leads to tremendous growth. As mentioned in the last chapter, consistency really is key.

What I've found through my training is that most people don't appreciate consistency as much as they should. Most join the gym, work out for a month, don't see immediate results, and then quit. I once saw an ad for an exercise machine. They advertised that if you used their machine for twenty minutes a day, three days a week, for six weeks, then you'll be the next supermodel.

> **There are no victories at bargain prices.**
> –General Eisenhower

Do the math: they are arguing that it only takes six hours of exercise to see remarkable differences. I don't agree. Most want to see results now, and most will only put in effort if they see an instant result, but this is not how team momentum works and it's not how personal development works. This kind of growth takes time and consistency, and that only happens when we work on it daily.

Entry-level employees don't get promoted in the first week. They recognize that they must be consistent in their daily activities to advance. They come to work on time every day. They fulfill their job responsibilities every day. They communicate with others and build relationships every day. The most effective entry-level employees who want to climb the ladder will also learn every day, and they've got a plan to do so.

Consider the amazing facts about the Chinese bamboo tree. Once a seed is planted, you will water and take care of the seed on a daily basis. After one year, you'll see no growth. The same goes for years two, three, and even year four. However, because you were consistent and did not give up, on year five, the tree will grow ninety feet in one single year. This is the power of consistency, and consistency is created through our daily actions.

Yourself Hold Accountable.

Learning does not make any impact unless you decide to do something with it. This last step of the growth plan is really more of a question: What are you going to do with your new learning?

How will you implement these new skills? What will you stop, start, or continue?

Learning for the sake of learning is a wasted act. Learning in order to grow, to become something more, to increase in capacity so that you can do more, be more, and help more is far from wasteful.

If you've been studying discipline or time-management techniques, what are you going to do next? Will you implement three daily actions after reading a book in the next two weeks? If you've been learning about communication skills, will you share with a member of your family four things you learned from listening to TED talks on communication?

I was taught early in my life to read good books. So, I read good books. In fact, I've read a lot of good books, but to be honest, I've not received nearly as much as I should have out of most of the books I've read. I read books because I felt like it was the right thing to do or because I wanted to say that I've read this book, or that book, or have read x number of books this month. It's as though I followed all of the DAILY steps but skipped the Y, and therefore, the true learning did not follow. In other words, I did all the work but didn't apply anything and therefore did not increase much in terms of my capacity.

I don't read that way anymore. I've learned that life is too short and that I should invest my time more wisely. When I read now, I read with a pen in my hand, I underline, I write in the margin, and I list ideas that come to my mind on the blank pages in the back. When I finish a book, I write a summary, I share what I've learned with at least one other person, and I put at least one idea into immediate action. Following this procedure, I learn a lot more, and I change, grow, and increase in capacity.

By following these five steps, you can become much more intentional in your daily learning and development. One of the greatest and best-known French writers was Victor Hugo, who wrote:

> He who every morning plans the transactions of the day and follows out that plan carries a thread that will guide him through the labyrinth of the busiest life. The orderly arrangement of his time is like a ray of light which darts itself through all his occupations. But where there is no plan, where the disposal of time is surrendered to the chance incidents, the chaos will soon begin.

Influential leaders develop and live by an Intentional Growth Plan to ensure learning and avoid chaos. Additionally, as they do this, they further equip themselves to grow the capacity in others.

BUILDING THE CAPACITY OF OTHERS

Up to this point of the chapter, the focus has been on you and developing your capacity. This has been deliberate, because you can't give or share something you don't have. However, if the only reason that you are increasing your capacity is to make yourself better, you'll soon lose motivation. Learning and increasing our capacity is hard work, and it requires a great amount of motivation to keep working on ourselves daily.

> *Before becoming a leader, success is all about growing yourself. When you are a leader, success is all about growing others.*
> –Jack Welch

While there are many ways to motivate yourself to learn, I've found that one method supersedes all the others. This method has been infused throughout this book in principles such as OB4S, the hammer principle, being significant in our service, and caring to confront. If you can center your efforts on this method, you'll tap into a never-ending spring of energy and motivation. You'll deepen your joys, strengthen your determination, and have a greater sense of purpose.

The best method for renewing your motivation is this: live to help others become intentional in building their own capacity.

Oprah Winfrey had it right when she said, "Helping others is the way we help ourselves." When we build others, we feel good. We get satisfaction. We become happier, and when this happens, we gain the motivation to keep building ourselves.

Allow me to illustrate with the following true story. In 1888, a French newspaper editor had mistakenly confused two brothers and printed an obituary for the wealthy and successful living brother, rather than for the dead one. You can imagine the living brother's surprise when he opened the newspaper and began reading about his own life as though he were dead.

"The Merchant of Death Is Dead," the headline proclaimed.

The article then went on to describe a man who had gained his wealth by producing products designed to kill people.

Not surprisingly, he was deeply troubled by this glimpse into what his legacy might have been, had he actually died on that day.

It is believed that this incident was pivotal in motivating him to change from developing his own capacity to developing the capacity of others. He took nearly his entire fortune and started a fund that encouraged people to do work that benefited humanity.

Even to this day, his organization considers advancements and improvements across the globe and then, every year, awards one person whose work surpasses the positive impacts of everyone else. You may have heard of this award, for it was named after its creator, Mr. Alfred Nobel—who was also the inventor of dynamite.

> **The function of leadership is to produce more leaders, not more followers.**
> –Ralph Nader

If you think success is determined by how far you have developed your capacity, you are wrong, and I hope you don't need a mistaken obituary to help you see this. Famed businessman Harvey Firestone asserts, "It is only as we develop others that we permanently succeed."

Norman Vincent Peale, author of the classic *The Power of Positive Thinking*, adds, "The man who lives for himself is a failure; the man who lives for others has achieved true success." As I've stated before, real success comes when we make the switch from focusing on ourselves to focusing on others.

This book would not be complete without a call for us to make it our mission to develop the capacity of others, for this is what true leadership is all about.

Character is important, because it attracts people to you. Building confidence is important, because it helps people feel good. Connecting is valuable, because it gives you the permission to go deeper into a person's life. And collaboration helps people accomplish more, and they will follow you for this. Yet, the very highest, the noblest, the number-one reason that draws the most commitment from people is when they follow you because of what you've helped them *become*. Building capacity in others helps them become a better version of themselves.

Monthly, for my church responsibilities, I meet one-on-one with my superior, who exemplifies this concept. He has been a tour guide for my leadership for many years, and I can come to him with any question.

In one instance, I had been trying to work with a particular individual for quite a while without any progress. My superior was so committed to my success that we lined up a home visit with this person. He then made the forty-five-minute drive south to spend an hour showing me how to work with people in such situations.

He really cared about my success and invested in me by providing to me tools, experience, and strategies to help me with specific challenges. He lives by the famed mantra "If you give a man a fish, you'll feed him for a day. If you teach a man how to fish, you'll feed him for a lifetime." He has helped me become a better me, and for that, I'll do almost anything he asks.

BEWARE OF DELEGATION

To build the capacity of others, you must first work with them to identify areas to grow in. Most organizations understand this need and have thus formally developed an assessment as part of their yearly evaluations. You probably are familiar with conducting performance evaluations with others. Some of these evaluations are great, while others are large and cumbersome (such as the one for Minnesota principals that has sixteen core areas and one hundred competencies).

Whether you have a good evaluation or not, what I have noticed is that even though most organizations have formalized the process of evaluation, they often do a poor job of developing people following the evaluation. In other words, they have identified needs and areas for growth but don't take the necessary, intentional steps to help foster that growth.

It's like they are telling their employees, "You are good at A, B, and C, but not so great at E and F. Keep working hard, and we will check back in a year to see if you are better at E and F," and then they place the evaluation into a file, only to be opened again in one year. This is not developing capacity.

Another mistake that I think many leaders make in developing capacity is their use of delegation. They mistakenly think, "If I want to help someone grow, I should delegate to them."

Let's be honest—what do you think of when you first hear the word "delegation"? I think of times when my parents "delegated" vacuuming, taking out the trash, and cleaning the bathroom as a way to "build character." No matter what my parents said, I could only see this as them passing down to me the things that they didn't want to do.

I've been in several situations where the leader I was working for delegated tasks to me. Instantly, I knew they were passing on what they didn't want to do. They took no thought as to what I needed. They had no true interests in growing me. They simply wanted to reduce what was on their plate and justified it by saying, "You have to start with this stuff so you can move up."

I'm not saying all delegation is bad; we have to delegate. You've heard, "delegate or die." It's true. Failure to do so incapacitates our ability to get all done that we need to do. Nor am I saying that we don't have to do things that are unpleasant; often, we have to do menial tasks before we can take on larger responsibilities, such as learning character from our parents.

What I am saying is that I don't like the word "delegate" because of how it is often handled: typically, in the form of pushed-down, simple, and repetitive tasks, for which there has been little thought and certainly no consideration as to how it can help build someone's capacity.

Merely passing on undesired tasks without thought to the needs of the other person is not developing capacity. No, I don't encourage delegation; rather, I prefer the empowering of others.

THE POWER OF EMPOWERING

To empower others is to make them stronger and more confident. It means to give them more control and power over their lives, their actions, and the lives and actions of others. When I think of empowering, I go back to my days as a teacher. I felt it my mission to help high-school students realize their abilities and potential through my belief in them and the challenges that I would ask them to complete.

> The ultimate use of power is to empower others.
> –William Glasser

Empowering gives people confidence. Empowering gives people responsibility. Empowering gives people the ability to make a difference. Certainly, there is a lot of power in empowering.

Contrary to delegation, empowering is not something you just do. It takes time and effort. Empowering begins with a strong desire to help someone grow and learn. It requires us to get to know the person that we'd like to empower, to know his or her strengths, weaknesses, and exactly what the person needs.

Empowering is when we use this knowledge to identify specific tasks or duties that will best match the strengths of the individual, while challenging the person to grow. Empowering is an intentional process, and it takes time, but the benefits of it can be absolutely incredible.

Empowering begins with identifying the potential individual to empower. If you are a leader over one person, this is a simple task. You are called to empower this person. However, if you lead a team, you'll need to determine who you are going to invest in.

Beginner leaders will say that they want to invest in all of those that they lead, and they can do this by using the first four rules of leadership described in this book.

However, rule five requires a wealth of time and commitment. This is not something that you can do for everyone at one time. You must be strategic in your time and investments. When considering whom to empower, rate the person on a scale of one to ten on the following fourteen points. Find an expanded version of these questions at www.i2eyesquared.com/resources under Assessment of Current Leadership Qualities.

Leadership Qualities

1. This person has good self-discipline.
2. This person communicates well with others.
3. This person has strong self-confidence.
4. This person has strong people skills.
5. This person has the ability to handle stress.
6. This person has a willingness to serve others.
7. This person embraces change.
8. This person can see the big picture.
9. This person doesn't give up easily.
10. This person lives by their morals.
11. This person understands others.
12. This person is positive.
13. This person has a strong sense of integrity.
14. This person has a desire to learn.

The second step to empowering others is to determine the need. Once you have identified the person to empower, it's time to sit down for a conversation.

First, explain that you've considered a lot of people and that you've chosen him or her as the person that you'd like to invest more time and effort in. If done well, this will boost his or her self-confidence (see rule two).

Second, ask for permission. Don't make the mistake of thinking that you're going to empower that person without his or her knowledge or consent. This should be an intentional process, and both of you should agree that you are going to work together to increase his or her capacity.

Third, go back to the section in this chapter on developing an Intentional Growth Plan. Walk through each of the **DAILY** steps to help that person develop a viable IGP. This is critical to helping you understanding how to empower your mentee.

Are you starting to see the difference between delegation and empowering others? Delegators don't align their tasks to the desires of others, while empowerers get to know the interests, wants, and needs of those they empower.

The fourth step of empowering is assigning a task. Here, too, we become intentional in our assignment and support for the task.

A few years ago, I had an interesting experience when my nine-year-old son Ethan asked me to empower him with the task of mowing the lawn. This is a request that he'd made for a few weeks, and although most dads would jump at this opportunity, I couldn't.

Having grown up in Utah, I'd developed strong opinions about lawn care. This may sound a little contradictory, as Utah is a desert. Lawns don't do well in a desert climate. Perhaps it's driven from a desire to have one green thing in the forest of brown, but when it comes to lawns, Utahns are extremely meticulous.

During my high-school and college years, I mowed lawns in the summer. I knew what it takes to ensure that all the lines are straight, to create an extremely sharp edge, and to leave the lawn looking like a well-groomed baseball field. Therefore, when a nine-year-old boy asked to take over my job, I was quite hesitant. Maybe this is how you feel when thinking about passing on duties and tasks to others—you know that you can do the job with great proficiency but question the ability of the person you're thinking of empowering.

> *Few things can help an individual more than to place responsibility on him, and to let him know that you trust him.*
> —Booker T. Washington

Luckily, my better judgment got to me, and I decided to pass this skill onto Ethan. After sitting down with him and explaining to him in great detail exactly how to mow, I let him loose.

You can imagine my surprise and shock when I came to inspect his finished job. There was not a single straight line. Parts of the lawn had been ignored. Grass was thrown all over the walkways, and he committed the cardinal sin of lawn mowing: crisscrossing the entire lawn to get the mower back into the shed! I was devastated.

If I were delegating, I would have simply taken back the task and would never give it to him again. But I'm empowering. Therefore, I quickly calmed down and went on a walk through the yard with him, showing him what he had missed, what he needed to correct, and how he could do better the next time.

Since we work with humans, there will be disappointments. They will not live up to our standards and will do things in ways that we know won't work. Yet, herein lies the power of empowering. This gives us a remarkable opportunity to help them grow and develop.

THE FIVE ELEMENTS OF EMPOWERING

Once we have identified the individual, have developed an IGP with the trainee, have determined a task, and are ready to assign the task, I have found that if we pay a FEE, the person will increase in capacity more quickly, and we will have fewer disappointments. FEE stands for the Five Elements of Empowering and I briefly describe each of these below:

1. *Do it.*

The tour-guide principle tells us that if we are to teach someone to do something, then we first must be proficient in the task. This step is a matter of competency. I would not have been able to teach Ethan to mow a lawn unless I was able to do so myself.

2. *Teach it.*

As a teacher, there were many times when I gave students instructions and asked them to get started, and then they fumbled. Often, the problem was that I didn't show them how something could be done. If you teach something new, ensure that you schedule time to model the task from the very start to the finish. Show them how to do it and let them watch you.

3. *Monitor it.*

Now it's time to turn it over to the person you are empowering. However, do not do as I did with Ethan. I followed steps one and two, but then I walked away, assuming he had learned. Great empowerers will stand by and coach the individual that is attempting something new.

Caution: the biggest mistake of leaders on this step is to think that their way is the only right way, and that may not be true. Avoid this mistake by suggesting how to do something and then easing back if they'd like to try it differently. They may find a method that is better than yours, or they may fail. Either way, the empowered person benefits.

4. *Authorize it.*

Most leaders, once comfortable, will allow the other person to individually complete the task. However, the temptation here is not to give complete authority. The temptation is to hold the power back so that if something does go wrong, you can quickly step in and take back control. Empowering is giving complete and total authority to the individual for a task.

When we hired our very first counselor for the junior high school, I determined several tasks that this person would be doing. I followed steps one through three and then told the staff that the new counselor would be responsible for the tasks.

In the following weeks, several requests came to my desk for things that I had empowered my counselor to do. I could have done these. Instead, I asked the individual to go to the counselor, as that was the person with the power to act and make decisions in the area of question.

Another temptation when working on this step is to micromanage. Don't. If you've done steps one through three well, then it's time to step back. You've provided the authority, so let that person make the decisions.

5. *Replicate it.*

Most will miss this step, but this is where real growth is. In short, you've not tapped into the power of empowering until the person you've empowered starts to empower others. That's a lot of empowering!

Take Ethan, for example. Two years later, he taught his younger brother how to mow the lawn. I have never given his brother instructions, yet he is now the primary person who mows, and he does a good job.

Asking people you've taught to teach another multiplies your organization's capacity and ability. Furthermore, as Roman philosopher Seneca asserts, "While we teach, we learn." Asking those that we empower to empower others causes both to become more empowered.

Since this book is about increasing influence, allow me to explain what empowering means in terms of your influence.

I decided to pay this FEE (to follow the Five Elements of Empowering) with a veteran teacher whom I will call Misty. We saw great potential in Misty, so we moved her from a teaching role over to an assistant principal role.

While it took a lot of time to empower Misty through several tasks and duties, I experienced tremendous returns on that investment of time. Not only was she more skilled and more capable of doing her job, but our relationship also moved to a higher level. Because of the time I took to invest into her, we developed more trust, more rapport, and more care for each other. Due to this, she often came to me for advice on major life decisions and allowed me to assist her in making positive impacts in her life through my influence. In other words, since I paid the price to help Misty increase her capacity, my influence with her increased. Furthermore, through our relationship, she has also had great influence on me.

She has now exceeded me in position and is doing some amazing things in the area of special services for the school district.

As I reflect on our relationship, the term *nachas* comes to mind. *Nachas* is a Yiddish term that means pride and satisfaction that is derived from someone else's accomplishment. *Nachas* is what you will get when you help increase the capacity of others.

Some might worry that if they invest into another, the other may leave. I think that Zig Ziglar summarized this nicely when he said, "The only thing worse than training employees and losing them is not training them and keeping them." Decide now to be a tour guide and help increase the capacity of those you serve.

BECOMING A TOUR GUIDE

☐ **Develop an Intentional Growth Plan (IGP).** If you don't currently have an Intentional Growth Plan, stop now and make one. Take the time to consider each of the five elements in the DAILY strategy. Don't skip this step. Invest in yourself, and really identify what you want and how you are going to get it. Find a template at www.i2eyesquared.com/resources.

☐ **Review the Performance Assessment.** Dig into your files and find a recent performance evaluation for a person you lead. Review the areas of improvement and resolve to do something to help that person in at least one area.

Name of person: _____

Area for improvement: _____

What will you do to help them grow in this area? _____

_____

☐ **Help Develop Another's IGP.** Using the DAILY strategy or the online template, help someone you serve develop an IGP. Discover where they would like to grow. Help them develop action steps that can be followed daily. Ensure you get their permission and that you have a plan for accountability.

☐ **Pay the FEE for Someone.** While it may take some planning to identify and help someone start an IGP, you can start changing how you ask people to do things by using the Five Elements of Empowering method now. If you have kids, this is a great place to practice. If you don't, identify a talent, hobby, or skill that you'd like to teach a friend and follow the FEE method to do so.

LIFE ON THE OTHER SIDE

*The highest reward for a person's toil is not what they get for it,
but what they become by it.*

—John Ruskin

NOT WHAT YOU EXPECTED

What I've realized through my experiences and working with many leaders is that life on the other side is not what you expect. I don't know what image comes to your mind as you see yourself leading, but perhaps it's like what I had in mind. Me, smoothly leading teams, having clear vision, speaking confidently, making things happen, being a mover and a shaker, and relishing in every moment as I gather a strong team of followers who put me on the map as an excellent leader.

While I am a firm believer that we need to project a positive image in our head and that what we think about will come about, let me also express that it is definitely not going to be as easy as you think.

President Teddy Roosevelt expressed, "Anyone who imagines that bliss is normal is going to waste a lot of time running around shouting that he has been robbed. Most putts don't drop. Most beef is tough. Most children grow up to be just people. Most successful marriages require a high degree of mutual toleration. Most jobs are more often dull than otherwise … Life is like an old-time rail journey—delays, sidetracks, smoke, dust cinders, and jolts, interspersed only occasionally by beautiful vistas and thrilling bursts of speed."[1]

You see, working with adults is messy business. As you lead people, you'll quickly realize that they are fickle, quirky, and often petty. Adults are just grown-up kids but with larger and more fragile egos. Honestly, it's hard to predict in a given day who is going to act like a whiny, sniveling, irritable baby and who is going to be a mature, clear-thinking adult.

Your job as a leader is to make people uncomfortable, and this runs counter to their comfort-seeking innate desires. People can get pretty upset when you take them outside their comfort zones.

Furthermore, most of the hard decisions, most of the tough conversations, most of the demands that require great courage will be done when you feel completely alone.

On the other side, there is often no one coming to save you, no handbook that gives you all the answers, and you'll frequently feel like you are simply making things up as you go along, all the while trying to portray a great deal of confidence on the outside. Leading others is not going to be what you expect.

THE PRICE OF THE OTHER SIDE

To complicate matters even more, the price that it takes to both get to and to stay on the other side is high. You're going to have to make sacrifices. You're going to have to give up your time. You're going to have to put your agenda behind the agenda of others. You're going to have to endure criticism and hardships. And, as one training participant recently stated, "you can't just show up to work and have fun anymore, because you've got this new responsibility on your shoulders."

Truly, when it comes to leadership, it is going to be hard work. Your personality, your connections, and your education will only get you so far. Hard work is what will really make you successful as a leader.

Truett Cathy, founder of Chick-fil-A, said that "the number-one reason leaders are unsuccessful is their inability to lead themselves." I'll add that they fail to lead themselves due to their unwillingness to put in the work that is required and to do it consistently until they become successful.

Author Seth Godin said, "We need to stop shopping for lightning bolts. You don't win an Olympic medal with a few weeks of intensive training, and there's no such thing as an overnight opera sensation. Great law firms and design companies don't spring up overnight ... Every great company, every great brand, and every great career has been built in exactly the same way: bit by bit, step by step, little by little." And every one of those steps requires work.

Many of us are looking for the quick jump, the shortcut up the ladder, the easy highway to successful leadership. However, my friends, these simply don't exist. Successful leadership is doing the hard things day after day, week after week, month after month, and year after year, despite the hardships, challenges, and failures.

> Leaders aren't born, they are made. And they are made just like anything else, through hard work.
> –Vince Lombardi

Probably the greatest author of all time in this area is the famed Napoleon Hill, whose classic 1937 text *Think and Grow Rich*, asserts that "Most of us are good 'starters' but poor 'finishers' of everything we begin. Moreover, people are prone to give up at the first signs of defeat. There is no substitute for persistence. The person who makes 'persistence' his watch-word will discover that 'Old Man Failure' finally becomes tired and makes his departure. Failure cannot cope with persistence."[2]

The price of the other side is nicely described in this short story: Not long ago, a middle-aged lady bought a ticket for a piano concert that was coming to town. She looked forward to this concert with great anticipation, as she is a lover of the piano and spends hours each day listening to the Classics.

When the day finally arrived, she was in complete bliss as she listened to a true master. For nearly 90 minutes, he tickled the ivories like no one else, and afterward, she stood with great vigor, applauding with all her might expressing her appreciation for a job well done.

Then, to her surprise, he came out of the backstage and started greeting the guests. Quickly, she found herself in line to shake hands with this wonderful pianist.

As they coupled hands, she expressed, "Gosh, I sure wish I could play as well as you do."

"Lady, no, you don't," he responded.

Shocked, she restated her first statement, "No, I do really wish that I could play as well as you do."

Again, the piano great responded, "No, you don't."

Suddenly, the ecstasy of the concert was replaced with an almost angry feeling, "No, you don't get it. I love the piano and really do wish that I could play as well as you do,"

> **It's hard to beat a person who never gives up.**
> –Babe Ruth

"I'm sorry, lady; I'm not trying to be rude, but it is actually you who doesn't get it."

He went on, "You see, twenty years ago, I started practicing for six hours a day, every single day. If you really want to play as I do, then tomorrow, you'll sit down at your piano and start playing for six hours and continue to do so every single day. Then, in twenty years, I guarantee you that you will be as good as or perhaps even better of a pianist than I am."

This pianist knew the price of the other side, because he's paid it. He got to be great through hard work and persistence. The sad truth is that most do not recognize nor understand the hard work and persistence that is required to make one great.

Yes, life on the other side is not going to be what you expect, and it is going to require more of you that you expect, **but it will be worth it.**

THE REWARDS OF THE OTHER SIDE

Ralph Waldo Emerson said, "It is one of the most beautiful compensations of this life that no man can sincerely try to help another without helping himself." When you cross to the other side and start serving others through your leadership, not only do you end up helping a lot of people, but you also help yourself. Here are five valuable lessons that leadership teaches.

1. *Being a leader teaches you trust.*

A leader's job is impossible to do alone. As you empower others, you learn to put your trust into others, expecting that they will complete what you can't. Sure, some will disappoint, but in my experience most will not.

2. *Being a leader helps you become comfortable being uncomfortable.*

Leaders learn quickly that the comfort zone is the enemy. Leaders must act, make hard decisions, and give critical feedback. All of this takes courage, and it requires you to live in the zone of discomfort.

3. *Being a leader teaches you patience.*

Although a powerful attribute of leadership is a drive to get things done quickly, you'll recognize that things will not be as quick as you hope. Working with people requires leaders to develop patience with both the processes and the growth of people.

4. Being a leader helps you see the big picture.

Technicians are great at seeing the day-to-day picture, but leaders must see how all the parts, all the people, and all the processes work together to create something beautiful. Leaders simply see more than others do. They develop a greater perspective that helps them to not be as bothered by the little things.

5. Being a leader teaches you who you are.

More than anything else, being a leader will force you to recognize and accept who you are. You can only fake it and survive in leadership for so long, and I suggest don't even try to fake it. Eventually, you must really get to know who you are: your interests, your desires, your values and morals, your motivations, your strengths, and your weaknesses. The sooner you come to this understanding, the quicker you'll learn about you.

Mahatma Gandhi said, "The best way to find yourself is to lose yourself in the service of others." There is nothing that helps you do this more quickly than being in the spotlight twenty-four hours a day, seven days a week.

Although these five leadership lessons should easily compensate you for your time, sacrifice, and efforts on the other side, there is one more thing that compensates even greater.

Leading others allows you to change lives. Leading others gives you a position of influence that, if used correctly, can allow you to have a significant positive impact on the lives of those you serve. Author Alan McGinnis says, "There is no more noble occupation in the world than to assist another human being—to help someone succeed."

There is no greater compensation for leadership than watching how your efforts help others to grow, develop, and live at a higher level. Leading others gives you the opportunity to help others win.

HELPING OTHERS WIN

Since most of my immediate family still lives in Utah, almost every year, we pack up the kids and make the drive to visit my family. A few years ago, our trip happened to be over the Fourth of July holiday. I was very excited about this. You see, every Fourth of July, the small town of Plain City has its annual 5K. I was a runner in high school and college, so I've run this 5K many, many times. In fact, I've won this race many times. So, when I realized that we'd be there for the race, I quickly signed my two boys and me up.

Now, I don't know about you, but whenever I go back home and encounter high-school friends that I have not seen in years, I feel like I have something to prove. Yes, I try to be a humble person as best as I can, but there's still something that gets into me around old high-school friends. Therefore, you can imagine how I felt when I looked a few years back on the winning times of this race and realized that I was in good enough shape to maybe win it.

It was 6:00 a.m., July 4th, and the gun is in the air. I've warmed up, I've checked out the competition, and I really do think I have a good shot of winning the race.

I look at my oldest son, Ethan, and he seems confident. He's a bit of a runner and has done 5Ks before. Then I turn and look to at my younger son Eli. There he stands, shaking and scared spitless. He has never even run three consecutive miles, much less competed in a 5K race before.

Right there, in a split second, I had a critical decision to make: do I move forward with my agenda, my hopes and dreams, everything that I want, or do I give it all up to help my son?

Well, I cannot say that I've always made the best decisions as a father, but at this moment, I chose to give it up and help him and for the next three long, grueling miles, I pushed, prodded, and encouraged my young boy to keep on running.

To my great surprise, he did and toward the finish line, I eased up to let him run ahead. As I watched him cross that finish line, I had the most wonderful, warm feeling come over me. I felt a joy so intense that it made me noticeably emotional. Because I gave up, because I sacrificed, I helped my boy have his own victory. I help him win.

Leadership is very much like this race. If we go into it focusing solely on our agenda and what we want, we may win the race, but we will miss the joy of helping others win.

Yet, if we humble ourselves and focus on the needs of others, if we sacrifice our desires to help others achieve their dreams, then we gain access to deep degrees of joy that cannot be found anywhere else in life.

This is why I wake up each morning. This is what convinces thousands of great leaders across the globe to keep doing the hard things. This is what drives people to step over to the other side and to use their new influence to make a profound positive impact on the lives of others. It's all about the joy of leading!

While I've certainly pointed out many of the challenges of being on the other side throughout this book, my greatest desire is that you've gained a hope. Hope that you can make a positive impact. Hope that you can model, motivate, and mentor others to live on a higher plane of life. Hope that you really can make a significant difference in this world and that the best way to do this is by leading through your influence.

Thank you for journeying with me through the Five Rules of Leading with Influence. I sincerely wish you the very best as you experience the amazing world of leading others.

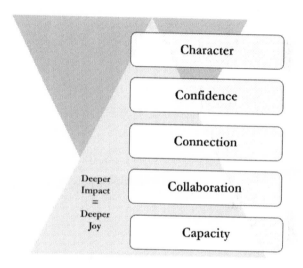

Acknowledgements

If someone would have told me how much time and effort it would take for me to write a book, I'm not sure I would have begun. This has been quite an experience and I could not have done it without the support of so many who surround me.

First and foremost, I must thank my amazing wife Sarah. Since the first time I considered leaving the security of a regular paycheck, she has supported me. She has been at my side through the ups and downs and holds a strong belief in my abilities. Honestly, if I didn't know she was supporting my every move, I would not be where I am today, and this book would simply have remained an idea.

It follows that I thank my kids second. They are a bunch of fun, energetic, and often crazy individuals who love their dad more than words can express. They have been patient with me, they take an active interest in both my writing and my business, and they keep asking me questions of what things will be like when I'm famous one day.

Next, I'd like to thank two of the humblest people I know, my parents Fred and Patsy Hunt. They were the ones that instilled in me many of the characteristics that I describe in this book. For that I will be eternally grateful. While we no longer live near my parents, I have had the fortune to be blessed with some outstanding nearby in-laws. Sincere thanks to my Minnesota parents Stephanie and Boyd Anderson, two of my biggest supporters.

I once read that a person will not be successful unless a lot of people want that person to be successful. I'm surrounded by many such people and wish to express my appreciation to those named below and the numerous others that will go unnamed who have made a difference in my life. Mike Redmond, my mentor in educational administration. Adam McDonald, a true friend of many years. Wendy Cirksena, who was my confidant during some hard times. John

Galbraith, my mission president who greatly influenced who I am today. Mark LaMaster a great support who has given me genuine friendship, time, and encouragement in writing a book. And finally, Mo (Gauher Mohammad), who from the first day we met has taken me under my wing, taught me almost everything I know about sales, and continues to challenge me both personally and professionally.

I have been a student of leadership and success principles for over twenty years, but no one has had such a deep and profound impact on my belief systems, my understanding of leadership, or my desire to add value to others as much as John C Maxwell has. John is truly a leader of leaders and while I am just one of many that he has influenced, my hope is that he will find satisfaction that he has added value to me, and in turn I am adding value to others.

I also wish to thank my two editors Stephanie Tillman and Dr. Charles K. Phillips. They have given great suggestions, have corrected all the little mistakes, and have made this book flow so much better than I could have on my own.

Finally, I wish to thank all of you, my readers. Thank you for having the belief in me that your time in this book will make a difference in your life. I know it will and hope that you have found great value through its teachings.

Notes

CHAPTER 1

1. Ralph M. Stodgill, *Handbook of Leadership: A Survey of Theory and Research* (New York, NY: The Free Press, 1974), 7.

2. Dwight D. Eisenhower, "Remarks at the Annual Conference of the Society for Personnel Administration", May 12, 1954. Online by Gerhard Peters and John T. Woolley, The American Presidency Project, http://www.presidency.ucsb.edu/ws/?pid=9884, accessed May 20, 2018.

3. English Oxford Living Dictionaries, s.v. "influence," accessed May 28, 2018 https://en.oxforddictionaries.com/definition/influence.

4. G.R. Stephenson, "Cultural acquisition of a specific learned response among rhesus monkeys," Progress in Primatology (Stuttgart: Fischer), 279-288.

5. "The Story Behind the Bus," The Henry Ford Museum, https://www.thehenryford.org/explore/stories-of-innovation/what-if/rosa-parks/, accessed May 20, 2018.

6. Donnie Williams and Wayne Greenhaw, *The Thunder of Angels: The Montgomery Bus Boycott and the People Who Broke the Back of Jim Crow* (Chicago Review Press, 2005), 48.

CHAPTER 2

1. Simon Sinek. *Start with Why* (London: Penguin, 2009), 85.

2. William A Gentry, Kristin L. Cullen and David G. Altman, Center for Creative Leadership, The Irony of Integrity: A study of the character strengths of leaders, https://www.ccl.org/wp-content/uploads/2015/04/IronyOfIntegrity.pdf, accessed May 16, 2018.

3. Sarah Amukhtar, Michael Gold, and Larry Buchman, The New York Times, *After Weinstein: 71 men accused of sexual misconduct and their fall from power,* https://www.nytimes.com/interactive/2017/11/10/us/men-accused-sexual-misconduct-weinstein.html, accessed May 18, 2018.

4. Watson Wyatt survey, "Work USA 2004/2005."

5. "Organizational Integrity Survey," KPMG, 2000 and New Employer/Employee Equation Survey, Age Wave and The Concours Group (New York, Harris Interactive, 2005).

6. Jessica Durando, "BP's Tony Hayward: I'd like my life back," *USA Today,* June 1, 2010, http://content.usatoday.com/communities/greenhouse/post/2010/06/bp-tony-hayward-apology/1#.W1sUU9IzqMo, retrieved May 24, 2018.

7. AT&T Code of Business Conduct, https://ebiznet.sbc.com/attcode/index.cfm#, accessed Feb 10, 2017.

8. From a 1997 survey of business executives by the Manchester Consulting Firm. John Sullivan, "Gain Trust by Being Consistent," *Tech Replublic,* April 29, 2002. Accessed July 22, 2009 https://www.techrepublic.com/article/gain-trust-by-being-consistent/.

9. Richard J. Maynes, "Earning the Trust of the Lord and Your Family," *Ensign,* November 2017, 22.

10. William A. Gentry, Todd J. Weber, and Golnaz Sadri, "Empathy in the Workplace: A tool for effective leadership," Center for Creative Leadership whitepaper, https://www.ccl.org/wp-content/uploads/2015/04/EmpathyInTheWorkplace.pdf, accessed May 25, 2018.

11. Bianca E. McCann, "Drive a High-Performance Organization with Empathy at the Core," https://www.betterworks.com/webinars/high-performance-organization-with-empathy/, accessed June 5, 2018.

12. Bear Bryant as quoted in John C. Maxwell, *Developing the Leaders Around You,* (Nashville, TN: Thomas Nelson, 1995), 2.

13. Melissa Bateson, Daniel Nettle, and Gilbert Roberts, "Cues of Being Watched Enhance Cooperation in Real-world Setting," *Biology Letters,* September 22, 2006, 412.

14. Sander van der Linden, "How the Illusion of Being Observed Can Make You a Better Person," *Scientific American*, May 3, 2011, https://www.scientificamerican.com/article/how-the-illusion-of-being-observed-can-make-you-better-person/, accessed Jun 5, 2018.

CHAPTER 3

1. Joe Robino, "The Impact of Lacking Self-esteem on Business Professionals," https://bodymindinstitute.com/the-impact-of-lacking-self-esteem-on-business-professionals/, accessed June 5, 2018.

2. Steven C. Marcus and Mark Olfson, "National Trends in the Treatment for Depression from 1998 to 2007," *Archives of General Psychiatry,* December, 2010, 1265-73 and Sally C. Curtain, Margaret Warner, and Holly Hedegaard, "Increase in Suicide in the United States, 1999-2014," *NCHS Data Brief No. 241,* April 2016

3. Steven R. Covey, *Principle Centered Leadership* (New York: Fireside, 1990), 173.

4. Winston Churchill.

CHAPTER 4

1. Daniel Goleman, *Focus* (New York: HarperCollins, 2013), 7.

2. R.P. Carver, R.L. Johnson and H.L. Friedman, "Factor analysis of the ability to comprehend time-compressed speech," *Journal of Reading Behavior,* Winter 1971-1972, 40-49.

3. Joanne B. Giordano, "Accenture Research Finds Listening More Difficult in Today's Digital Workplace," https://newsroom.accenture.com/industries/global-media-industry-analyst-relations/accenture-research-finds-listening-more-difficult-in-todays-digital-workplace.htm, accessed June 25, 2018.

4. R. Bandler and J. Grinder, *Les secrets de la communication: Les techniques de la PNL* (Paris: Le Jour Editeur, 1982).

CHAPTER 5

1. Peter Flade, Jim Asplund, and Gwen Elliot, "Employees Who Use Their Strengths Outperform Those Who Don't," *Gallup Business Journal*, October 8, 2015, https://news.gallup.com/businessjournal/186044/employees-strengths-outperform-don.aspx, accessed Jan 4, 2018.

2. Brandon Rigoni and Bailey Nelson, "Few Millennials Are Engaged at Work," *Gallup Business Journal*, August 30, 2016, https://news.gallup.com/businessjournal/195209/few-millennials-engaged-work.aspx, accessed June 5, 2018.

3. I.L Janis, "Groupthink," *Psychology Today*, April 1, 2010, 43-46.

CHAPTER 6

1. Jenkins Lloyd Jones, quoted in "Big Rock Candy Mountains," *Deseret News*, June 12, 1973, A4.

2. Napoleon Hill, *Think and Grow Rich* (Northbrook, IL: Random House), 100.

ABOUT THE AUTHOR

JASON HUNT is the founder and owner of Eye Squared Leadership, an organization that helps people make a profound positive impact in the lives of others through leadership development and team-building. Jason first crossed to the other side when he accepted an assignment to lead a congregation of sixty church members in outer Siberia at the age of nineteen and has been on the other side ever since. He has a master's degree in leadership from the University of Minnesota and is a certified John Maxwell Team Member. Jason lives in southern Minnesota with his wife, Sarah, and their four children, Ethan, Eli, Ande, and Esther.

To learn how Eye Squared Leadership can help you with your team's leadership needs, or if you would like to explore having Jason speak at your next event, please contact:

Eye Squared Leadership
730 22nd St SE
Owatonna, MN 55050
United States of America

Phone: 507-363-3842

E-mail: jason@i2eyesquared.com

Social: @i2eyesquared

www.i2eyesquared.com